Communication Mastery

The Science and Art of Transforming Communication

Skills for Success: A Step-by-Step Guide to Unlocking the Secrets to Effective Interpersonal Dynamics

Joseph Aminian

All Rights Reserved

No part of this book may be reproduced, or stored in a retrieval system, or transmitted in any form or by any means, electronic, mechanical, photocopying, recording, or otherwise, without express written permission of the publisher.

ISBN (paperback): 978-1-0689910-8-0
ISBN (eBook): 978-1-0689910-9-7
ISBN (PDF): 978-1-0691459-0-1

First Edition Published November 2024

© Copyright 2024 Joseph Aminian

Table of Content

INTRODUCTION	9
CHAPTER 1	11
THE FOUNDATIONS OF EFFECTIVE COMMUNICATION	11
CHAPTER 2	25
MASTERING THE ART OF LISTENING	25
CHAPTER 3	43
DECODING NON-VERBAL COMMUNICATION	43
CHAPTER 4	61
CULTIVATING EMPATHY IN INTERACTIONS	61
CHAPTER 5	80
STRATEGIZING HIGH-STAKES COMMUNICATION	80
CHAPTER 6	97
READING BETWEEN THE LINES	97
CHAPTER 7	115

ADAPTING COMMUNICATION STYLES FOR SUCCESS 115

CHAPTER 8 135

HARNESSING EMOTIONAL INTELLIGENCE 135

CHAPTER 9 152

FREUDIAN SLIPS AND SPEECH PATTERNS: CLUES TO UNDERLYING THOUGHTS 152

CHAPTER 10 169

APPLYING COMMUNICATION SKILLS IN BUSINESS CONTEXTS 169

CONCLUSION 185

REFERENCES 190

Introduction

In an increasingly interconnected world, the ability to communicate effectively can be your most powerful asset. "Communication Mastery: The Science and Art of Transforming Communication Skills for Success" is your essential guide to harnessing the full potential of verbal and non-verbal dynamics.

This book breaks down complex communication concepts into clear, actionable strategies, blending science with the art of human connection to help you excel personally and professionally. Whether you're a business leader, sales professional, or simply someone seeking self-improvement, this step-by-step guide empowers you with proven techniques to elevate every interaction.

In today's fast-paced world, the stakes in communication are high. From navigating critical business negotiations to deepening personal connections, your success hinges on how well you understand others and, ultimately, how well they understand you. This book provides you with transformative skills to become a masterful communicator, guiding you in deciphering underlying messages and adapting your approach for the best possible outcomes. You'll uncover methods to foster trust, encourage openness, and ensure that your messaging resonates with people in meaningful ways.

Through targeted techniques and real-world applications, "Communication Mastery" enables you to refine your listening, bolster your emotional intelligence, and project empathy. These essential skills will empower you to engage confidently in high-stakes professional settings, elevate client relationships, and enhance interpersonal connections across all areas of life.

Are you ready to turn every interaction into an opportunity? Let this book guide you toward the unparalleled power of effective communication—your path to impactful, lasting success begins here.

Joseph Aminian

November 1, 2024

Chapter 1

The Foundations of Effective Communication

Effective communication is a crucial skill that extends far beyond the exchange of words. It involves a complex dance between conveying thoughts clearly and understanding others, helping to build solid foundations for relationships both in professional and personal spheres. The importance of mastering communication is evident across all forms, from verbal exchanges to nuanced non-verbal cues like body language and tone. As we navigate our daily interactions, these elements work together to form a seamless flow of information that fosters connection and collaboration, unveiling communication as both an art and a science.

In this chapter, readers will embark on a detailed exploration of the fundamental principles governing successful communication. Through an examination of various models, the chapter highlights how different processes influence the effectiveness of message delivery and reception. By understanding these frameworks, such as the Linear, Interactive, Transactional, and Contextual Models, individuals can refine their communication strategies for clarity and adaptability.

The chapter also delves into recognizing and overcoming common barriers to effective communication, including physical, psychological, semantic, and cultural obstacles. Furthermore, the role of context is analyzed to illustrate how situational, cultural, relational, and historical factors shape communication dynamics. For business professionals, self-improvement enthusiasts, and sales and marketing experts alike, this comprehensive guide serves as a blueprint for enhancing interpersonal skills, fostering stronger relationships, and achieving professional success through improved communication practices.

Definition and Importance of Communication

Communication is a vital component in our daily interactions, serving as the bridge between individuals and groups. At its core, communication is about exchanging information and fostering meaningful connections, whether through words, gestures, or expressions.

Verbal communication involves spoken and written words, enabling us to convey our thoughts clearly and precisely. Non-verbal communication, on the other hand, includes body language, facial expressions, and tone of voice, often revealing emotions and intentions that words alone cannot express. Together, these elements form a comprehensive system that allows people to understand and be understood, making communication both a science and an art.

In professional settings, effective communication is particularly significant. It establishes the foundation for strong relationships, promotes collaboration, and enhances teamwork. When team members communicate openly and honestly, they build trust and respect with one another. This dynamic leads to a more cohesive work environment where ideas can be freely shared, fostering innovation and problem-solving. For instance, in a brainstorming session, participants who actively listen and provide constructive feedback create an atmosphere of mutual support that encourages creativity and collective growth.

Moreover, polished communication skills are fundamental to career success and leadership credibility. Professionals who articulate their thoughts confidently and adapt their communication style to suit different audiences are often perceived as competent and trustworthy. Leaders with such skills inspire their teams, ensure clarity in their directives, and manage conflicts effectively.

Consider a manager who holds regular team meetings to discuss progress, address concerns, and celebrate achievements. By doing so, they not only maintain transparency but also boost morale and productivity, reflecting the positive impact of strong communication on organizational success.

However, the absence of effective communication can result in misunderstandings, conflicts, and missed opportunities. Poorly articulated messages may lead to confusion, causing errors and delays in project execution. Misinterpretations can escalate tensions among colleagues, resulting in conflicts that disrupt the workflow and damage professional relationships.

An example of this could be an email sent without proper context, which might be misread as critical rather than constructive, leading to unnecessary friction. Furthermore, a lack of clear communication in client interactions might result in lost business opportunities, as potential clients may feel undervalued or misunderstood.

Guidelines for improving communication skills are essential for professionals seeking to enhance their effectiveness in the workplace. First and foremost, active listening is crucial. By paying close attention to what others are saying, one can respond thoughtfully and avoid misunderstandings.

Additionally, being mindful of non-verbal cues such as eye contact and gestures can help reinforce verbal messages and demonstrate engagement. Practicing empathy is another key aspect, which involves considering others' perspectives and emotions when communicating. This approach helps in building rapport and resolving conflicts amicably.

Effective communication also requires adaptability. Professionals should be flexible in their communication styles, tailoring their messages to suit different contexts and audiences. For instance, the way one communicates with a casual colleague over lunch will differ from how one addresses a board meeting.

The ability to adjust tone, language, and formality makes communication more relatable and impactful. Moreover, providing and seeking feedback regularly can enhance communication practices, allowing individuals to refine their skills continuously.

Measuring communication effectiveness is important for ongoing improvement. One way to do this is by setting specific, measurable goals related to communication, such as increasing team participation in meetings or reducing email response times. Gathering feedback from peers, managers, and clients can offer valuable insights into how one's communication is perceived and areas for development. Self-assessment tools and reflection exercises can also aid in identifying strengths and weaknesses in communication habits.

Models of Communication Processes

Exploring the frameworks of communication requires delving into models that shed light on how information exchange operates. One such model is the Linear Model, which focuses on a straightforward sender-message-receiver flow. This model highlights potential delivery failures within communication, emphasizing the importance of the sender accurately transmitting a message and the receiver clearly understanding it. The linear approach underscores the simplicity yet fragility of communication, where any disruption in clarity or noise can lead to misunderstandings.

The Interactive Model then expands on this by incorporating feedback loops and context into communication dynamics. Unlike the linear model, the interactive model allows for two-way exchanges, acknowledging the role of feedback from the receiver. This interaction creates a more dynamic process where both participants actively influence each other's responses.

Context plays a crucial role here, as it encompasses physical, psychological, and situational elements that affect how messages are constructed and interpreted. For instance, a conversation in a professional setting may carry different meanings depending on factors like workplace culture or individual stress levels, illustrating the necessity of understanding these layers for effective communication.

In contrast, the Transactional Model illuminates simultaneous communication, where every participant acts as both sender and receiver, creating a constant flow of meaning.

This model stresses that communication is not merely about exchanging information but involves collaborative shifts influenced by emotions. Participants are engaged in creating social realities together, signifying that communication shapes relationships and perceptions continuously.

For example, in a business meeting, non-verbal cues like facial expressions and tone of voice contribute to this ongoing transaction, affecting how messages are received and acted upon. It illustrates that communication is not just about words but also about interpreting emotional undertones and intentions, fostering a deeper connection among individuals involved.

Another layer of understanding is provided by the Contextual Model, which emphasizes how individual backgrounds shape interpretations and empathy in exchanges. This model considers the profound impact of personal experiences, cultural norms, and historical contexts on communication practices. Individuals bring their own worldviews to interactions, which can create diverse interpretations of the same message.

For instance, what might be considered a straightforward directive in one culture might be seen as overly direct or even rude in another. Recognizing these differences enhances empathy and adapts communication styles to suit varied audiences. In sales and marketing, this understanding is paramount, as crafting persuasive messaging requires insight into clients' diverse perspectives and needs.

The exploration of these communication frameworks provides valuable insights into how professionals can enhance their interpersonal skills. Each model offers a unique lens through which to understand the intricacies of communication. By identifying potential pitfalls in message delivery, as highlighted by the linear model, professionals can refine their methods for clarity and precision. Embracing the dynamic nature of the interactive model fosters adaptability, encouraging professionals to adjust approaches based on feedback and contextual cues to achieve desired outcomes.

Simultaneously, the transactional model's focus on emotional influences and collaborative meaning-making elevates communication strategies, particularly in team settings where building rapport and understanding is essential for success. Finally, the contextual model reminds us of the importance of acknowledging diverse backgrounds and fostering empathy, critical for creating inclusive and respectful communication environments.

For business professionals aiming to improve networking and client interactions, recognizing these frameworks empowers them to tailor messages effectively, ensuring alignment with organizational goals and audience expectations. Self-improvement enthusiasts can leverage these insights to nurture personal growth, developing emotional intelligence by appreciating feedback and adapting to various contexts. Sales and marketing professionals benefit greatly from these models, as understanding the nuanced transaction of communication aids in refining techniques for better client engagement and retention.

Barriers to Effective Communication

In the realm of communication, understanding the barriers that obstruct effective exchange is essential. These barriers, if left unaddressed, can undermine both personal and professional relationships. Identifying these obstacles not only helps in recognizing their existence but also in developing strategies to overcome them.

Physical barriers are perhaps the most tangible and most straightforward to address. Distance and noise are prime examples. Whether it's a team scattered across different continents or a busy office with constant interruptions, physical barriers can be quite detrimental. The advancement of technology has largely mitigated these issues. Video conferencing tools such as Zoom or Teams have shrunk distances, allowing for seamless face-to-face communication without the need for co-location. Strategic planning also plays a key role; scheduling regular check-ins or using noise-cancellation techniques in office setups are practical steps to bridge these gaps effectively.

Psychological barriers, on the other hand, delve deeper into the human psyche. Emotional interference and biases can cloud judgment and disrupt communication. Emotions, while vital for authentic interaction, often lead to misunderstandings if not managed properly. A person may approach a conversation with preconceived notions or emotional turmoil, hindering open dialogue.

Mindfulness and emotional intelligence are crucial tools in addressing these barriers. Awareness of one's emotional state and practicing empathy towards others can significantly enhance communication effectiveness. Before engaging in important conversations, taking a moment to evaluate emotional readiness can help prevent miscommunication. Emotional intelligence facilitates this process by encouraging individuals to understand and manage their emotions better, thereby fostering clearer communication.

Semantic barriers arise from language differences and jargon. In today's global society, diverse languages and specialized terminologies can create confusion. This is especially true in digital communication, where the lack of vocal and visual cues can exacerbate misunderstandings. Simplifying language and encouraging questions are simple yet powerful strategies in overcoming semantic barriers.

By avoiding unnecessary jargon and opting for clear, concise language, communicators can ensure their messages are easily understood by all parties. Encouraging feedback opens the floor for clarification, allowing recipients to ask questions and confirm their understanding, which reduces the potential for misinterpretation.

Cultural barriers are another significant area of concern in communication. As people from diverse backgrounds interact more frequently, cultural differences can pose challenges. These differences might include variations in customs, values, or even non-verbal cues. Such barriers can impede effective communication if not addressed appropriately. Developing cultural competence is essential in overcoming these barriers.

Cultural competence involves understanding and respecting differences, which in turn fosters an inclusive environment for communication. Cultivating respect for different perspectives and being open to learning about various cultures can enhance interpersonal relations and facilitate smoother interactions. For example, acknowledging different cultural norms regarding eye contact or personal space can drastically improve mutual understanding and cooperation in multicultural teams.

Role of Context in Communication

Understanding how context shapes communication is crucial for effectively navigating interactions, whether in personal or professional environments. Context provides the backdrop against which messages are sent and received, influencing meaning, interpretation, and outcomes.

Situational context plays a pivotal role in how we tailor our messages. This aspect of context involves being aware of the specific circumstances surrounding a communication act. For instance, consider the differences in communication style required at a bustling trade show compared to a quiet one-on-one meeting in an office. The urgency, formality, and overall tone need adjustment based on these situational cues. In emergencies, clear and concise communication is paramount. Likewise, job interviews demand a formal approach, focusing on qualifications and role fit. Each situation requires us to adapt our messaging to meet the expectations and needs inherent in that particular environment.

Cultural context broadens this perspective by urging communicators to consider the diverse backgrounds of their audience. Every culture has distinct norms, values, and communication styles. An effective communicator recognizes these differences and modifies their approach accordingly.

For example, what might be considered a straightforward comment in one culture could be perceived as rude in another. By adapting communication styles to suit diverse audiences, deeper connections are fostered. In multicultural workplaces or international dealings, understanding cultural nuances can mean the difference between success and misunderstanding. By acknowledging cultural identities—such as race, gender, and nationality—communication becomes more inclusive and effective, thus respecting individual perspectives and experiences.

Similarly, relational context refers to the dynamics between individuals engaged in communication. Relationships vary widely, from close-knit friendships to hierarchical workplace structures. Trust levels and familiarity influence how messages are interpreted. For instance, feedback from a trusted colleague might be welcomed, while the same input from someone less familiar could be met with skepticism. Understanding these relational dynamics helps in crafting messages that resonate well with the recipient's perceptions. Trust built over time not only facilitates open dialogue but also enhances the efficacy of the communication itself.

Historical context, meanwhile, invites us to assess past interactions and how they inform present communication. Every dialogue carries with it the weight of previous encounters. Recognizing patterns or repeating themes aids in providing continuity and understanding in ongoing communications.

A business relationship that has evolved over years will reflect shared experiences and mutual history, which subtly shape current exchanges. Learning from past communication failures or successes guides individuals and organizations toward more refined strategies. This appreciation for history enriches dialogues, making them more relevant and meaningful. These contextual elements work together to craft the art and science of communication. While each holds its own significance, they are often intertwined, influencing one another. Situational cues may intersect with cultural understandings, just as relational histories may color how current messages are interpreted within certain environments. An informed communicator recognizes this interplay and adapts accordingly, thus becoming adept at navigating complex communication landscapes.

In practice, this means constantly honing awareness and sensitivity towards the various contexts of communication. Business professionals seeking to enhance their networking skills must be particularly attuned to these dynamics. Effective client interactions depend heavily on understanding both personal and broader cultural contexts. Similarly, self-improvement enthusiasts will find that developing such awareness significantly boosts their emotional intelligence. As for sales and marketing professionals, mastering persuasive communication involves grasping these context clues to better engage and retain clients.

The key to leveraging context is active listening and observation. By being fully present in each interaction, individuals can pick up on subtle cues that indicate the prevailing context. Whether it's recognizing a client's cultural preferences or noting changes in team dynamics, these insights inform strategic communication decisions. Over time, building this contextual intelligence becomes second nature, allowing adaptability and responsiveness in varied communication situations.

Bringing It All Together

In this chapter, we explored the fundamental principles that make communication both a science and an art. We've covered how various forms of communication—verbal and non-verbal—connect us to others and enable us to convey thoughts and emotions effectively. Understanding these elements helps enhance relationships in professional environments by promoting trust, collaboration, and innovation. We also examined the significance of polished communication skills in leadership, where adapting styles to different audiences can inspire confidence and resolve conflicts. Recognizing the barriers, such as physical or psychological challenges, and developing strategies like active listening and empathy are essential for overcoming communication obstacles.

Furthermore, diving into the models of communication processes provided insights into how these exchanges operate. From the Linear Model's simplicity to the Interactive, Transactional, and Contextual Models' complexities, each framework highlighted unique aspects of communication dynamics. By acknowledging these models, professionals can refine their communication methods, tailor messages to diverse audiences, and adapt to various contexts for better interactions. This understanding equips business professionals, self-improvement enthusiasts, and sales and marketing specialists with the tools needed to enhance interpersonal skills, foster meaningful connections, and drive career success.

Chapter 2

Mastering the Art of Listening

Mastering the art of listening is more than just hearing words; it's about attentively engaging in conversations to uncover deeper meanings and foster connections. Listening, often overshadowed by speaking, holds the power to transform everyday interactions into meaningful exchanges. In an era where effective communication is pivotal for personal and professional growth, developing attentive listening skills becomes crucial. Business professionals, self-improvement enthusiasts, and sales experts alike can benefit from honing this skill, which forms the foundation of insightful engagement in both personal and work-related environments.

Throughout this chapter, the distinction between active and passive listening will be explored, shedding light on how each style impacts dialogues and relationships. Readers will discover techniques to balance these approaches, making them adaptable communicators in various scenarios. Practical exercises and real-life examples will illustrate the significance of utilizing active listening in settings like team meetings or client negotiations.

Additionally, the chapter delves into the nuances of emotional cues and how non-verbal signals enhance understanding. By identifying common listening pitfalls and learning strategies to overcome them, readers will be equipped to navigate complex conversations with empathy and precision. The insights provided aim not only to improve listening abilities but also to elevate interpersonal dynamics across diverse contexts, fostering lasting connections and professional success.

Active vs Passive Listening

In the world of communication, listening is often overshadowed by the art of speaking. Yet, the capacity to listen actively or passively can significantly influence the effectiveness of interactions, whether they involve casual exchanges or crucial business meetings. Distinguishing between active and passive listening is vital, as each serves different purposes and impacts dialogue in unique ways.

Active listening is a dynamic, engaging process where the listener fully participates in the conversation, paying close attention to both the words spoken and the underlying messages conveyed through tone and nonverbal cues. Active listeners provide feedback, ask clarifying questions, and use verbal affirmations such as "I see" or "That's interesting," which not only enhance the speaker's confidence but also deepen the dialogue's richness.

For example, in a team meeting, an active listener might say, "Could you elaborate on that point?" This shows interest and encourages further discussion, ensuring clearer comprehension and minimizing misunderstandings.

Conversely, passive listening is more reserved and involves receiving information without expressing outward reactions or engaging with the speaker. This style can be suitable in situations where absorbing information is critical, such as during lectures or when the content is less relevant personally.

However, it often leads to missed nuances and potential misunderstandings due to the lack of engagement with the speaker. For instance, in a busy work environment, someone might listen passively to a colleague discussing weekend plans. Here, the listener absorbs just enough information for later reference but doesn't engage deeply because the conversation context isn't crucial.

A balanced approach, combining both active and passive listening techniques, allows for adaptability and nuanced comprehension within conversations. In scenarios where detail and thorough understanding are paramount, like client negotiations or resolving conflicts, active listening plays a dominant role.

However, knowing when to switch to passive listening can prevent cognitive overload and allow individuals to conserve energy for moments demanding acute focus. An adaptable listening style is especially beneficial in diverse environments, such as multicultural teams, where listening needs may fluctuate based on cultural norms and expectations.

Real-life scenarios and roleplays offer practical insights into the application of these listening styles. Consider a scenario in customer service, where an agent encounters a dissatisfied client. Active listening becomes crucial here; by attentively acknowledging the client's concerns and asking targeted questions, the agent demonstrates empathy and commitment to resolving the issue. This, in turn, fosters trust and can lead to more positive outcomes. On the other hand, imagine a classroom setting where a student needs to absorb a lecture's content without interacting with the teacher. Here, passive listening enables the student to efficiently gather necessary information without engaging in continuous discourse.

Roleplaying exercises can be instrumental in refining these skills, enabling individuals to experience different listening scenarios and recognize the appropriate style to employ. In a workshop setting, participants might practice switching between active and passive modes, simulating real-world situations like networking events or board meetings. These exercises help illustrate the impact of listening choices on communication effectiveness.

The distinction between active and passive listening is not merely academic but holds practical relevance across various professional spheres. Business professionals seeking to refine their communication skills will find that mastering when to listen actively versus passively can significantly enhance team dynamics and client interactions, fostering more meaningful relationships.

Similarly, self-improvement enthusiasts dedicated to personal growth can leverage these listening techniques to develop deeper emotional intelligence and improve interpersonal connections. Moreover, sales and marketing professionals can utilize active listening strategies to better understand client needs and build lasting engagements through attentive, responsive communication.

Techniques for Focused Attention

In the bustling world of business and personal interactions, mastering the art of attentive listening can be transformative. Keeping concentration during conversations is vital for genuinely understanding and engaging with others, particularly for professionals seeking to enhance interpersonal communication skills. By adopting mindfulness practices, setting clear intentions, creating a distraction-free environment, and employing reflection techniques, individuals can significantly improve their focus and comprehension.

Mindfulness practices are a powerful tool for enhancing concentration by minimizing distractions and managing intrusive thoughts. To practice mindfulness, one might start by incorporating simple exercises into daily routines. For instance, mindful breathing—focusing solely on each breath entering and leaving the body—can help center the mind and reduce stress (Mayo Clinic, 2020). This focused breathing acts as a reset button, bringing attention back to the present moment, which is crucial during intense discussions or negotiations.

Additionally, setting clear intentions before engaging in conversations can markedly enhance focus and foster proactive engagement. Before beginning a meeting or dialogue, taking a moment to contemplate the desired outcome can align one's energy and attention towards achieving that goal. Setting an intention could be as straightforward as aiming to understand the other party's perspective or striving to find common ground. Such premeditated focus not only hones attention but also encourages meaningful contribution, facilitating more effective and enriching exchanges.

Equally important is creating an environment conducive to deep listening, free from distractions that may disrupt the flow of conversation. This includes turning off electronic notifications, choosing a quiet location, and ensuring all parties feel comfortable and undistracted. In a professional setting, this might mean organizing meetings in calm, neutral spaces or utilizing soundproof rooms to minimize background noise. Indeed, fostering such an environment not only aids concentration but also signals respect and commitment to those involved, thereby improving understanding and rapport.

To reinforce comprehension and identify areas for improvement, reflection techniques after conversations are invaluable. Taking time to mentally replay the dialogue can illuminate gaps in understanding or highlight parts of the conversation that require further exploration. Reflection could involve jotting down key points or feelings evoked during the exchange.

Guided journaling post-conversation is another method, encouraging introspection and yielding insights into personal listening patterns or biases. This ongoing practice helps in ingraining lessons learned, refining listening strategies, and preparing better for future engagements.

Ultimately, the fusion of these practical techniques fosters not only enhanced listening skills but also stronger relationships built on trust and empathy. In business contexts, this translates to improved networking capabilities, more effective client interactions, and strengthened team dynamics.

A sales professional, for example, benefits immensely from active listening, as it enables them to tailor pitches that resonate with clients' specific needs, therefore boosting engagement and retention. Business executives who listen attentively often find themselves better equipped to address team members' concerns, ultimately cultivating a more cohesive and motivated workforce.

On a broader scale, these practices encourage personal growth and emotional intelligence development. They teach individuals to remain present, appreciate diversity in perspectives, and engage empathetically with colleagues and friends alike. By integrating mindfulness and intentional focus into daily life, one embarks on a journey of self-improvement, paving the way for more fulfilling interpersonal relationships and successful career trajectories.

Listening for Emotional Cues

In today's fast-paced world, the ability to understand and interpret emotional cues in conversations is a skill that can lead to more meaningful interactions. Emotional cues often extend beyond spoken words, revealing underlying sentiments and intentions. Recognizing these cues can alter how messages are received, fostering empathy between individuals. To achieve this, it is essential to consider several key aspects.

First, understanding the emotional tone of a conversation can significantly affect the interpretation of its message. Emotional tone refers to the feeling conveyed through words and non-verbal communication such as gestures and facial expressions.

For instance, a statement made with a light-hearted tone may be interpreted differently than the same statement delivered with a harsh or sarcastic tone. Recognizing these variations helps in altering our perception of what is being communicated. By understanding the emotional tone, listeners can respond more appropriately, thereby fostering a sense of empathy and connection with the speaker.

Empathy is a cornerstone of effective listening. When we listen empathetically, we validate the feelings of others, creating an environment where they feel heard and understood.

Empathetic listening involves more than just absorbing words; it requires attention to emotional undertones that give depth to spoken language. A supportive interaction atmosphere is cultivated when listeners reflect back not only the content but also the emotions behind what is being said. This reflects a deeper understanding and encourages open and honest communication.

Non-verbal modalities play a crucial role in deciphering these emotional cues. Body language, for example, often reveals emotions more accurately than words alone. Crossed arms might indicate defensiveness, while a relaxed posture can signal openness and receptivity.

Similarly, facial expressions can quickly convey emotions like surprise, anger, or happiness, sometimes even before the speaker is aware of them. Being mindful of these non-verbal signals allows us to gain a more comprehensive understanding of the speaker's emotional state.

The power of body language can be demonstrated through practical activities that enhance the interpretation of these cues. Activities such as "Mirror, Mirror," where individuals mimic the body language of others to better understand their feelings, can sharpen observational skills and highlight the impact of non-verbal communication on interpersonal dynamics (Selby, 2023).

Another useful exercise is emotion charades, which involves acting out various emotions without using words, thus helping participants appreciate the subtleties of non-verbal expression and interpretation.

In professional settings, interpreting emotional signals correctly can strengthen team dynamics, improve client relations, and enhance overall communication strategies. For business professionals and sales teams, understanding the emotional landscape of conversations can directly impact networking success and client retention. Appreciating the emotional context of a discussion can help in crafting persuasive messages that resonate on a deeper level.

To further develop skills in recognizing and interpreting emotional cues, incorporating mindfulness practices into daily routines is beneficial. Mindfulness encourages individuals to slow down and fully engage with the present moment, making them more attuned to subtle emotional signals during interactions.

Setting clear intentions for each conversation can guide focus and enhance participants' ability to stay engaged and responsive, ensuring distractions do not cloud their observations.

Additionally, eliminating distractions from the environment can enable better concentration and comprehension. In today's interconnected world, multitasking often leads to divided attention and diminished listening capabilities. Creating spaces free of distractions helps in maintaining focus, allowing individuals to better understand both verbal and non-verbal cues within conversations.

These techniques not only improve personal relationships but are also invaluable in professional contexts, where emotional intelligence can prove to be a competitive advantage. By enhancing one's emotional intelligence through empathy and active engagement, individuals can navigate complex social and professional landscapes with greater ease.

Finally, practical exercises provide an opportunity to apply these skills effectively.

Role-playing scenarios that involve interpreting emotional signals offer a hands-on approach to learning, allowing individuals to practice and refine their responses in controlled environments. These exercises cultivate a sensitivity to emotional nuances, enabling participants to develop more authentic connections in real-world situations.

Avoiding Common Listening Pitfalls

In the realm of effective communication, mastering the art of listening is crucial for fostering meaningful interactions. Despite its importance, numerous hurdles impede our ability to listen effectively. Recognizing these barriers and actively developing strategies to overcome them can enhance both personal and professional exchanges.

One of the most common obstacles in effective listening is interruptions during conversations. Whether they stem from others or ourselves, interruptions break the flow and derail our focus. To counteract this, it's important to adopt techniques that encourage maintaining silence while others speak.

Practice active listening by nodding or using brief verbal affirmations like "I see" or "Go on," which signal that you are engaged without disrupting the speaker. Patience in these situations demonstrates respect and allows for a more complete understanding of the message being conveyed.

Another significant hurdle is prejudging speakers or their content before they've fully expressed themselves. This tendency to make assumptions obstructs genuine engagement.

When we approach a conversation with preconceived notions, we filter what we hear through those biases, often missing out on valuable insights.

Instead, approach each interaction with an open mind. This doesn't mean abandoning critical thinking, but rather suspending judgment until you've absorbed the full context. By doing so, you pave the way for richer dialogue and learning opportunities.

A prevalent issue in many listening scenarios is the focus on formulating a response rather than truly understanding the speaker's message. This shift in attention occurs because we're eager to express our own thoughts.

However, it reduces the depth of our understanding of what's being communicated. A solution lies in consciously slowing down our thought processes. By prioritizing comprehension over crafting a reply, we hone our ability to grasp the nuances of the speaker's message. In doing so, we foster more thoughtful and informed responses that contribute to a more meaningful exchange.

Personal distractions are another major impediment to effective listening. These distractions can range from internal worries to external stimuli, all competing for our attention during conversations. Self-regulation plays a vital role here, requiring us to mentally tune out unrelated thoughts and focus intently on the speaker.

Developing this discipline involves practicing mindfulness techniques, such as deep breathing before engaging in a conversation, or briefly summarizing the speaker's points in your mind. These methods anchor our attention, allowing us to remain present and receptive. Reflection techniques offer an additional layer for enhancing listening skills. After a conversation, take some time to reflect on what was said and how it was received. Consider questions like: "What key themes emerged?" and "Did I fully understand their perspective?"

Engaging in this reflective practice not only reinforces the information received but also identifies areas where listening could be improved. For instance, if you notice a pattern of interrupting, acknowledging this allows you to consciously curb the habit in future interactions.

Additionally, empathy is a powerful tool in overcoming listening barriers. Approaching conversations with empathy means striving to understand the emotional undertones behind words. This doesn't suggest assuming emotions but rather being attentive to cues that may hint at unspoken feelings. By validating these emotions, we create an environment where speakers feel heard and respected, facilitating a more genuine connection.

Practicing empathy involves asking clarifying questions not only about facts but also about how the speaker might be feeling regarding the topic discussed. This builds trust and openness, encouraging further sharing and deeper understanding.

Balancing Listening Approaches

In the pursuit of mastering complex subject comprehension, achieving a balance in listening approaches is paramount. This subpoint focuses on integrating listening techniques to enhance understanding and engagement in conversations. By blending active listening into seemingly passive moments, we can transform mundane exchanges into rich dialogues that foster deeper comprehension.

Active listening is often seen as a deliberate, effortful process requiring full attention and thoughtful feedback. However, by incorporating elements of active listening even during less demanding, passive interactions, we elevate the quality of these encounters.

For instance, simple actions like maintaining eye contact, nodding in affirmation, or asking clarifying questions can turn an ordinary chat into an opportunity for meaningful dialogue. These subtle cues signal engagement and encourage participants to share more openly, resulting in a more comprehensive exchange of ideas.

Roleplaying scenarios serve as a vital technique to demonstrate the power of adaptive listening styles across different contexts. Such exercises allow individuals to practice pivoting between listening modes depending on situational needs. In a professional setting, for example, roleplays can simulate negotiations where one must oscillate between assertive and receptive listening based on conversation dynamics. This flexibility ensures that all information is adequately processed, paving the way for more informed decision-making.

Consider a scenario where team members are role-playing a customer service call. The listener may have to switch from actively engaging with the customer's immediate concerns to passively absorbing background details that could inform a broader strategy. Roleplaying these shifts enhances one's ability to navigate real-world situations effectively, underscoring how adaptive listening supports diverse conversational objectives. As noted by Martins (2022), active listening exercises hone communication skills crucial for both personal and career growth.

Sharing anecdotes of successful conversations further illustrates the tangible benefits of active listening. Take, for example, a story of a project manager who regularly practices active listening with their team. By genuinely focusing on each member's input without interruption or preconceived judgments, this manager fosters a collaborative environment where innovative solutions emerge organically. Team morale improves, productivity rises, and projects consistently meet deadlines, showcasing the direct impact of attentive listening (Martins, 2022).

Such stories not only inspire but also provide concrete evidence of active listening's efficacy. They highlight how attentive engagement leads to better outcomes, reinforcing its value in both personal relationships and business settings. Furthermore, they serve as motivational evidence for those striving to enhance their interpersonal communication skills.

Adapting listening styles to various professional contexts is another crucial step in mastering complex topics. Business professionals, especially, must recognize when to employ different listening approaches to suit specific environments. For instance, sales executives often need to decipher client needs quickly and accurately. Here, active listening becomes indispensable. By tuning into verbal cues and emotional nuances, salespeople can tailor their pitches to strike a chord with potential clients, increasing the likelihood of successful deals (Mind Tools, 2022).

Similarly, marketers banking on consumer insights must adeptly shift between researching trends (passive listening) and engaging directly with customers (active listening) to craft effective campaigns. Tailoring their approach allows them to tap into genuine consumer desires while developing strategies that resonate on a deeper level. This adaptability emphasizes that the art of listening extends beyond mere hearing; it involves understanding context and responding appropriately.

Business professionals and self-improvement enthusiasts alike benefit from lessons found in providing space for dialogue evolution. Allowing conversation flow without rushing transitions invites broader perspectives and encourages true comprehension of complex subjects.

This patience, married with good listening practices, opens doors to unexplored insights and strengthens interpersonal connections. Finding the right rhythm between listening styles can profoundly enhance how we interact, learn, and grow—professionally and personally.

Bringing It All Together

Developing strong listening skills is essential for interpreting the underlying messages in any conversation, as discussed throughout this chapter. We've explored how active listening promotes engagement by incorporating feedback and questions, ensuring clear understanding and minimizing misunderstandings. On the other hand, passive listening allows for information absorption without immediate interaction, making it useful in contexts like lectures or less critical discussions. By blending both styles, individuals can adapt to different conversational situations, fostering more nuanced communication.

Furthermore, implementing practical techniques such as setting intentions before interactions and creating distraction-free environments enhances focus and comprehension. Mindfulness practices, like focused breathing, help maintain attention during intense discussions, while reflection techniques provide opportunities to assess and improve listening habits.

Recognizing emotional cues through tone and body language further deepens our connections with others, adding empathy to our interactions. By mastering these listening strategies, both business professionals and personal growth enthusiasts can achieve more meaningful relationships, ultimately enhancing their effectiveness within professional and personal realms.

Chapter 3
Decoding Non-Verbal Communication

Decoding non-verbal communication involves understanding the subtle yet powerful cues that extend beyond spoken words. As we navigate our daily interactions, body language, facial expressions, and vocal tones play critical roles in shaping perceptions and conveying unspoken messages. These elements offer insights into others' thoughts and emotions, often revealing more than verbal communication alone can express.

To connect effectively with others, it is vital to become attuned to these silent signals, which add depth and clarity to our interpersonal exchanges. By honing the ability to read and respond to non-verbal cues, individuals can enhance their communication skills, making interactions more meaningful and impactful.

This chapter delves into the various aspects of non-verbal communication, focusing on body language, facial micro-expressions, and vocal nuances. It explores how mastering these skills can improve professional and personal interactions, benefitting business professionals, self-improvement enthusiasts, and sales experts alike.

You will discover practical applications for interpreting gestures and expressions, as well as techniques to refine vocal delivery for optimal impact. Additionally, the chapter addresses the importance of cultural awareness in understanding non-verbal cues across different contexts. Through engaging examples and insights, this exploration aims to empower you to utilize non-verbal communication as a strategic tool in both your career and personal growth.

Understanding Body Language

Body language is a vital part of communication, revealing much about our attitudes and emotions through postures, gestures, and movements. Imagine a colleague enthusiastically gesturing during a meeting or someone crossing their arms while listening; these actions can speak volumes about their engagement, openness, or defensiveness. Mastering the interpretation of body language enhances our ability to connect with others, allowing us to read these silent signals accurately.

The universality of some non-verbal cues underscores their importance. For instance, a nod often indicates agreement, while a shrug might signify uncertainty. However, interpreting these gestures requires attentiveness to the context and cultural backdrop of the individuals involved. While a nod is generally understood as a positive response in many cultures, in Bulgaria, it might mean disagreement (Zucchet, 2023). Such variations highlight the complexities of non-verbal communication across different regions and emphasize the need for cultural awareness.

Understanding cultural dynamics is crucial because gestures that are benign in one culture may carry entirely different implications elsewhere. Take, for example, the "OK" sign made by forming a circle with the thumb and forefinger. In Western cultures, it typically signals approval, but in parts of Europe and South America, the same gesture can be offensive (How to Navigate Nonverbal Communication in Different Cultures, 2024). Engaging with diverse cultures necessitates being sensitive to these differences to avoid misunderstandings and foster mutual respect.

Consistency between verbal and non-verbal cues is another fundamental aspect of effective communication. When words align with gestures and expressions, they build trust and reinforce messages. An individual who says they are excited while maintaining an enthusiastic posture is more likely to be believed than someone who delivers the same message with a slouched stance and monotone voice. In professional settings, aligning these elements is particularly significant for leaders, as it increases credibility and authenticity.

For business professionals and those looking to enhance interpersonal relations, employing techniques to utilize body language effectively can greatly improve interactions and negotiations. Adopting open postures, such as uncrossing arms and maintaining eye contact, signals attentiveness and receptivity in conversations. These subtle gestures encourage the other party to feel valued and understood, paving the way for productive dialogue.

Navigating negotiations involves more than just persuasive speech; body language plays a critical role in conveying confidence and authority. Standing or sitting upright, using deliberate hand movements, and mirroring the other person's positive gestures can create a conducive environment for collaboration. Mirroring, which involves subtly copying the gestures or expressions of the other person, fosters rapport by creating a sense of empathy and shared understanding.

Practicing conscious control over one's non-verbal cues can also aid in managing one's presence and influence in various scenarios. In high-stakes meetings or presentations, ensuring that body language supports spoken content can significantly impact outcomes. For example, pacing one's speech with corresponding gestures can enhance clarity and keep the audience engaged.

Providing guidelines for interpreting body language is essential for maximizing its practical applications. Professionals can begin by observing how different cultures express themselves and practice adapting their non-verbal behaviors accordingly. This might mean consciously minimizing hand gestures when communicating with individuals from cultures where such movements are perceived as overly expressive or even aggressive.

Furthermore, honing observation skills is invaluable for accurately reading non-verbal signals. By paying close attention to small nuances in facial expressions and gestures, one can gain insights into the sentiments and intentions behind them. Regularly practicing this skill will strengthen the ability to decode these cues instinctively.

Training programs and workshops focusing on body language can offer structured learning experiences to deepen understanding and application of these techniques. Such training can provide opportunities for feedback and refinement, ultimately leading to enhanced communication efficacy.

Interpreting Facial Micro-Expressions

Facial expressions serve as a vital component of non-verbal communication, operating as a universal language that transcends the barriers of spoken dialects. These expressions provide insight into an individual's emotional state and intentions, helping us navigate social interactions with greater empathy and understanding.

Numerous studies have demonstrated that certain facial expressions are universally recognized across diverse cultures, thereby highlighting their significance in human communication. Research by Dr. Paul Ekman identified seven basic emotions expressed through facial movements: anger, fear, disgust, happiness, sadness, surprise, and contempt. For instance, a smile reflecting happiness is generally understood worldwide, just as a frown indicating anger or sadness conveys similar meanings across different cultural backgrounds. This universality facilitates empathy—a crucial element in building effective interpersonal relationships within both personal and professional realms.

Beyond these macro-expressions lie micro-expressions, which are brief, involuntary facial expressions revealing genuine emotions. Unlike more prominent expressions, micro-expressions can occur within a fraction of a second, making them challenging to detect. However, their fleeting nature makes them particularly valuable in high-stakes environments like negotiations or law enforcement. Micro-expressions can uncover underlying feelings such as anxiety or dishonesty even when someone attempts to mask their true thoughts. Recognizing these subtle cues can significantly enhance one's negotiation skills, enabling professionals to respond strategically based on the authentic emotions of others.

Furthermore, the interpretation of facial expressions alters the perceived meaning of verbal messages. Consider a scenario where a colleague delivers positive feedback with a stern face—the verbal message might be affirmative, but the accompanying facial expression could suggest sarcasm or insincerity.

Conversely, words of consolation accompanied by a warm smile and gentle eye contact amplify the feeling of empathy and care. Thus, understanding this interplay between facial expressions and spoken words is essential for achieving desired communication outcomes, especially in fields like sales and marketing, where maintaining client relations is paramount.

Improving one's ability to recognize and respond to facial expressions can elevate emotional intelligence, a trait increasingly valued in modern workplaces. Emotional intelligence involves discerning and influencing the emotions of oneself and others. By honing skills to accurately interpret facial expressions, individuals can more effectively manage their own emotions and navigate complex social situations. This practice encourages better awareness of how others perceive one's actions and words, fostering a more harmonious and collaborative environment.

To cultivate these skills, engaging in practical exercises focused on recognizing and responding to facial expressions is beneficial. One useful technique is through observational training, which involves watching videos or real-life interactions to identify various facial cues.

By noting the context and matching it with corresponding expressions, individuals can sharpen their ability to pinpoint specific emotions. Additionally, mirror exercises where one mimics different facial expressions can increase self-awareness of one's expressive capabilities, reinforcing the mind-body connection.

Role-playing scenarios with peers presents another opportunity to practice interpreting expressions in dynamic settings. This method allows participants to experience diverse reactions and receive constructive feedback. Understanding how others interpret your facial responses enables you to adjust them accordingly, making your interactions more effective and empathetic. Regularly incorporating these exercises into personal development plans can gradually enhance emotional perception skills, ultimately leading to improved social connections and communication proficiency.

In business contexts, mastering the art of decoding facial expressions offers competitive advantages. Being attuned to a client's unspoken feelings can guide professionals in tailoring their approach to suit the client's emotional state, promoting trust and long-term relationships. It empowers leaders to manage team dynamics effectively, identifying potential conflicts early and fostering a supportive atmosphere conducive to collaboration and innovation. For self-improvement enthusiasts, these insights contribute to personal growth, enriching interactions by adding emotional depth and authenticity.

Importance of Vocal Tone and Rhythm

Vocal qualities such as tone, pitch, and rhythm are integral to how messages are received and interpreted. Each aspect of vocal delivery plays a unique role in conveying emotions and shaping listeners' perceptions, which significantly impacts the communication process. By mastering these elements, one can improve overall communication effectiveness, whether in business meetings, personal interactions, or public speaking engagements.

Tone of voice is perhaps the most immediate indicator of emotion when we speak. It serves as an emotional barometer, hinting at underlying sentiments, like frustration, enthusiasm, or concern. For instance, a warm, inviting tone can foster trust and openness, essential for effective client interactions or team collaborations.

On the contrary, a harsh or dismissive tone could unintentionally create barriers, leading to misunderstandings or conflict. This dynamic demonstrates why being mindful of our tone is crucial. Emotionally charged words might not align with a speaker's intended message if the tone contradicts its purpose. Therefore, conscious modulation of tone in alignment with desired emotions can greatly enhance clarity and connection.

Pitch also carries substantial weight in speech delivery, influencing how listeners perceive messages. High-pitched voices often convey excitement or urgency, while low pitches might express seriousness or calmness. Business professionals, for instance, use variations in pitch for emphasis during presentations, ensuring key points resonate with their audience. Recognizing these subtleties can aid in adjusting one's pitch to match the context and emotion needed for different conversations, thereby enhancing the listener's understanding and engagement. Such adjustments can break the monotony in longer dialogues and keep audiences captivated.

The rhythm, or pace of speech, further affects how effectively a message is communicated. The speed at which someone talks influences both clarity and comprehension among listeners. Speaking too quickly may overwhelm recipients, causing key details to be missed, particularly in complex explanations or negotiations. Conversely, speaking too slowly can lead to disengagement as attention drifts. Striking a balance is essential; a deliberate pace helps maintain interest while allowing listeners time to absorb information thoroughly. Adapting rhythm to the listener's needs shows respect for their processing capabilities, strengthening interpersonal connections and fostering empathy.

Modulating your vocal delivery to suit different contexts is equally important. Contextual awareness involves tailoring your vocal approach based on situational demands. In a professional setting, expressing confidence through a steady, assertive voice can establish credibility and command respect. Meanwhile, softer tones reflecting empathy or understanding can be more appropriate in sensitive discussions or when delivering difficult news. This flexibility allows speakers to build stronger rapport with their audience by aligning their vocal expressions with the social or emotional context at hand.

For those aiming to master vocal techniques, practical exercises can immensely benefit their skill set. Engaging in vocal warm-ups prepares the voice for optimal performance, reducing tension and improving articulation.

Exercises like humming or lip trills help in loosening vocal cords and controlling breathing, leading to a smoother voice flow. Practicing mindful reading encourages understanding of how varying tones can alter a message's impact, offering insights into effective tonal shifts. Critical listening, where individuals record their own speech to scrutinize pitch, tone, and rhythm, can reveal personal patterns and areas needing improvement.

Role-playing scenarios provide another avenue for refining these skills. By simulating various conversational settings, individuals can practice adapting their vocal qualities to different audiences and contexts. This method builds comfort and adaptability, especially valuable for sales and marketing professionals who must engage diverse clients persuasively. Feedback from trusted sources or voice coaches offers objective perspectives, highlighting strengths and areas requiring refinement. This iterative approach ensures constant growth and adjustment in vocal delivery.

Micro-Gestures as Silent Communicators

Micro-gestures are an intriguing phenomenon in the realm of non-verbal communication. They are subtle, often involuntary movements that can reveal a person's subconscious thoughts and feelings. Unlike more obvious body language cues, micro-gestures occur on a much smaller scale, yet they play a crucial role in conveying emotions and intentions. Understanding these tiny movements can provide significant insights into the real sentiments behind a person's words, which is invaluable in both personal and professional interactions.

Common micro-gestures can indicate underlying emotions and intentions. For instance, a fleeting glance away during a conversation might suggest discomfort or a lack of confidence. A quick tap of the fingers could signal impatience or anxiety. These small actions, often unnoticed, can speak volumes about what someone is truly feeling, even if their verbal communication suggests otherwise. Recognizing these gestures aids in decoding the genuine emotions at play, enabling one to respond with greater empathy and understanding.

In high-stakes communication settings, such as business negotiations or important meetings, micro-gestures offer a layer of context that is essential for interpreting honesty or anxiety. During a negotiation, for example, a participant who exhibits micro-gestures like repeatedly touching their face or shifting their posture might be concealing stress or uncertainty. This observation provides an opportunity to address underlying concerns before they escalate. Conversely, a steady gaze and minimal fidgeting can project confidence and honesty, strengthening the trust between parties involved.

Developing sensitivity to micro-gestures enhances relational dynamics. It allows individuals to tune into the unspoken aspects of communication, promoting a deeper level of connection. By being attentive to these involuntary signals, people can react more appropriately and engage more meaningfully with others.

In leadership roles, this skill is especially beneficial; leaders who are adept at reading micro-gestures can gauge the morale and engagement of their team, providing necessary support or adjustments when needed. Implementing awareness of micro-gestures in daily interactions can create a more harmonious and effective workplace environment.

Implementing micro-gesture awareness improves team cohesion and collaboration. Teams that understand and recognize micro-gestures can communicate more effectively, as members become aware of each other's comfort levels and emotional states without explicit verbalization. This knowledge fosters an atmosphere where individuals feel understood and valued, leading to more productive teamwork. By paying attention to the subtleties of communication, teams can preempt misunderstandings and resolve conflicts more swiftly. This increased awareness also encourages open dialogue, as team members feel supported and acknowledged in their expressions, both verbal and non-verbal.

It's essential to develop strategies for recognizing and responding to micro-gestures in various contexts. One effective approach is through active observation, which involves consciously noting the micro-gestures of others during interactions. Practicing this skill can sharpen one's ability to detect these subtle cues over time. Additionally, seeking feedback from others regarding one's interpretations can help refine this skill further. Role-playing exercises can also be useful, allowing individuals to experiment with different scenarios and responses based on micro-gestural cues.

For those looking to enhance their professional competencies, workshops focused on micro-gestures can be particularly beneficial. Such training sessions often involve video analysis of interactions, where participants learn to identify micro-gestures and interpret their meanings accurately. These workshops provide practical experience, enabling attendees to apply their newfound skills in real-world situations. As a result, professionals become more adept at navigating complex interpersonal dynamics, whether in client meetings, team collaborations, or leadership scenarios.

While developing sensitivity to micro-gestures is key, it's equally important to recognize that cultural differences can influence these gestures. What might be considered a sign of nervousness in one culture could be interpreted differently in another. Therefore, cultivating cultural awareness alongside micro-gesture recognition is crucial. This dual focus ensures that misinterpretations are minimized, and interactions remain respectful and effective across diverse cultural contexts.

Practical Applications of Non-Verbal Communication

In our rapidly evolving communication landscape, mastering non-verbal cues is instrumental in enhancing our interactions. This chapter delves into the practical application of non-verbal communication skills, emphasizing their role in various contexts to improve both personal and professional engagements.

Awareness of one's own non-verbal behavior is foundational in shaping self-presentation and authenticity. By understanding how our body language, facial expressions, and tone of voice affect others, we can align our intentions more closely with our interactions.

For instance, maintaining eye contact can project attentiveness and engagement, which are essential in both professional meetings and personal conversations. Understanding cultural variations in non-verbal cues is also crucial; while direct eye contact is encouraged in some cultures as a sign of honesty and confidence, it may be deemed disrespectful or aggressive in others (Maaike Boer, 2022). Hence, cultivating awareness helps in adjusting our non-verbal behavior to suit varying social norms and expectations, thereby improving authenticity and connection.

Practicing mirroring and role-playing further refines our ability to interpret and apply non-verbal skills effectively. Mirroring involves subtly imitating another person's body language to build rapport and empathy. It's a strategy often employed in sales and negotiations to create an atmosphere of trust.

Role-playing scenarios can aid in honing these skills by simulating real-life interactions, allowing individuals to practice reading cues and adjusting their responses accordingly. For example, in a team meeting setting, practicing mirroring the leader's open posture or positive gestures can enhance group dynamics and demonstrate active participation.

Feedback sessions play a pivotal role in enhancing one's understanding of the impact of non-verbal actions on interactions. Constructive feedback from peers or mentors can highlight unconscious habits that may affect communication negatively, such as crossing arms during discussions, which can be perceived as defensive. By receiving and reflecting on such feedback, individuals can consciously modify their non-verbal signals to foster more positive and effective communication. In a workplace context, regular feedback sessions can help employees fine-tune their interpersonal skills, thereby boosting overall team performance and cohesion.

To deepen knowledge and application of non-verbal communication techniques, engaging in training and workshops proves invaluable. These educational settings provide structured environments where participants can learn about various aspects of body language, such as the significance of posture, gestures, and space management. Through interactive exercises and expert guidance, individuals can gain insights into advanced techniques like recognizing micro-expressions or adjusting vocal tones to convey emotion and clarity (Non-Verbal Communication - Key Interaction Skills and How to Improve, n.d.).

Workshops specifically tailored for business professionals can offer specialized training that aligns with career goals, such as effective client negotiation and networking strategies.

The importance of integrating these non-verbal communication strategies lies not only in their immediate applicability but also in their long-term benefits. For business professionals aiming to bolster their career trajectories, mastering non-verbal cues can lead to improved networking opportunities and enhanced client interactions.

For self-improvement enthusiasts, these skills contribute to developing emotional intelligence and fostering better relationships in all spheres of life. Sales and marketing professionals can particularly benefit by refining their persuasive messaging and building long-lasting client relationships through adept non-verbal communication.

One practical guideline for applying these lessons involves establishing a routine for self-assessment and improvement. Setting aside time each week to reflect on recent interactions and receive peer feedback can facilitate continuous growth in non-verbal communication. Additionally, seeking mentorship or coaching can provide personalized insights and strategies tailored to individual strengths and areas for improvement.

Moreover, it's vital to recognize the influence of technology on non-verbal communication. With virtual meetings becoming commonplace, understanding digital non-verbal cues, such as webcam framing and virtual eye contact, becomes increasingly important. Adapting traditional non-verbal skills to fit digital platforms ensures that communication remains effective, regardless of medium.

Bringing It All Together

This chapter has thoroughly explored the significance of non-verbal communication through body language, facial expressions, and vocal tone. Recognizing these elements allows us to connect more authentically with others, transcending the limitations of spoken words. By understanding how gestures, postures, and even micro-expressions reveal subconscious thoughts, we can better navigate diverse social situations and cultural nuances. This insight not only enriches personal interactions but is invaluable in professional settings, fostering trust and creating conducive environments for collaboration.

For business professionals, self-improvement enthusiasts, and sales experts, mastering these skills offers significant advantages. Employing effective body language techniques can enhance client relations, improve team dynamics, and cultivate personal growth. Techniques such as mirroring and feedback collection can be instrumental in refining one's approach to communication. Additionally, adapting these skills to virtual environments ensures that our interpersonal engagement remains effective, regardless of the medium.

As we integrate these powerful non-verbal tools into our everyday interactions, the potential for more meaningful and fulfilling relationships in all areas of life becomes increasingly attainable.

Chapter 4
Cultivating Empathy in Interactions

Cultivating empathy in interactions is essential for enhancing communication, fostering deeper connections, and building understanding among individuals. Empathy allows us to step into another person's emotional world, creating a bridge that leads to authentic relationships.

In the context of interpersonal dynamics, practicing empathy can transform superficial exchanges into meaningful dialogues where emotions are acknowledged and validated. As we navigate both personal and professional spheres, implementing empathy becomes a powerful tool for collaboration and effective communication. This chapter emphasizes how empathetic interactions can elevate the quality of relationships within diverse settings, illustrating the wide-ranging benefits of prioritizing empathy in our daily lives.

In this chapter, you will explore various dimensions of empathy, including its definitions, manifestations, and differences from related concepts like sympathy and compassion. The nuances of cognitive and emotional empathy will be examined, showcasing their significance in both personal and business environments.

Additionally, the chapter delves into practical techniques for cultivating empathy, such as active listening and open-ended questioning, which help enhance communication by encouraging open dialogue and mutual understanding. Overcoming barriers to empathy, recognizing biases, and appreciating cultural perspectives are also discussed as vital components in fostering empathetic interactions. This comprehensive exploration aims to equip readers with the skills necessary to build stronger interpersonal connections, whether they're seeking to improve networking, client relations, or nurture personal growth.

Defining Empathy in Communication

In the realm of communication, empathy serves as a cornerstone for developing genuine and meaningful connections. Empathy, at its core, is the ability to understand and share the feelings of others, creating a bridge between individuals that transcends mere words. Within communication contexts, empathy enables us to perceive the emotions and perspectives of those we interact with, thereby facilitating deeper understanding and rapport.

To truly grasp empathy's role in communication, it is essential to distinguish it from sympathy. Sympathy often involves feeling pity for someone else's situation and may distance us from their experience.

It lacks the shared emotional connection that empathy fosters. While sympathy might prompt you to send condolences to a grieving colleague, empathy encourages you to sit with them in their sorrow, acknowledging their pain and offering your presence.

This difference highlights why empathy is vital in building authentic relationships. It allows us to connect on an emotional level, demonstrating understanding and compassion rather than simply acknowledging another's distress.

Empathy manifests in various forms, one of which is cognitive empathy. Cognitive empathy, also known as empathic accuracy, refers to the ability to comprehend another person's thoughts and emotions. Unlike emotional empathy, which primarily deals with feeling what others feel, cognitive empathy involves perspective-taking or viewing the world through another's eyes.

This skill is invaluable in communication, especially in professional environments where understanding a client's needs or a team member's frustrations can lead to better collaboration and outcomes. By recognizing and intellectually understanding another's feelings, we can tailor our responses to meet their needs more effectively, enhancing mutual respect and cooperation.

On the other hand, emotional empathy involves not just understanding, but actually sharing another person's emotional state. It requires a personal connection to the emotions of others, contributing to experiences that are often richer and more profound. Emotional empathy goes beyond intellectual comprehension; it involves resonating with another's joy, sadness, or anger, making interactions vibrant and genuine.

For instance, when a co-worker shares good news and you feel their happiness ripple through you, that's emotional empathy at work. This form of empathy significantly impacts interpersonal relationships by promoting a sense of unity and belonging, fostering environments where people feel valued and supported.

While empathy can be a powerful tool in communication, it is important to exercise it thoughtfully. Over-identifying with someone's emotions can lead to personal distress, where boundaries between self and other become blurred.

Balancing empathy with self-awareness ensures that we remain supportive without compromising our well-being. Thus, understanding personal limits and practicing self-care are integral when employing empathy in interactions, allowing us to maintain healthy relationships while offering genuine support to others.

Techniques for Empathetic Engagement

Cultivating empathy in interactions is essential for establishing meaningful connections and nurturing understanding within interpersonal dynamics. One of the critical aspects of empathetic communication is active listening, which fosters an environment where empathy can thrive by concentrating entirely on the speaker.

When we engage in active listening, we are not merely hearing words but fully immersing ourselves in what the speaker is trying to convey. This means paying attention not just to verbal communication but also to nonverbal cues such as tone, body language, and facial expressions. Active listening requires creating a space where the speaker feels valued and understood. It involves setting aside distractions, maintaining eye contact, and using open body language to signal attentiveness.

By acknowledging the speaker's message through nodding or brief affirmations like "I see" or "I understand," we reinforce their feelings and encourage further sharing. Through this process, we demonstrate that we genuinely care about their experiences, concerns, and emotions, which is foundational in cultivating empathy.

Open-ended questions play a vital role in advancing deeper conversations and uncovering underlying emotions. Unlike closed questions that elicit short, often limited responses, open-ended questions invite the speaker to explore and express their thoughts and feelings more comprehensively.

Questions such as "How did that situation make you feel?" or "Can you tell me more about your experience?" prompt the speaker to delve into their emotions and perspectives.

These questions serve as gateways to discovering the nuances of an individual's experience. They encourage dialogue that goes beyond superficial exchanges, revealing the layers beneath initial responses. As speakers open up, they often articulate emotions that might not have been immediately apparent, helping both parties gain a richer understanding of the situation at hand. For business professionals, utilizing open-ended questions can lead to increased engagement and better problem-solving by tapping into client or team member insights.

Reflective responses further enhance empathetic communication by validating the emotions expressed by the speaker. Reflective responses involve paraphrasing or summarizing what the speaker has said, allowing them to hear their thoughts reflected back. This practice not only confirms that the listener has accurately understood the speaker's message but also shows that the listener acknowledges and respects their emotional state.

For example, if a colleague shares frustration about a challenging project, a reflective response might be, "It sounds like you're feeling overwhelmed by the demands of the project." This approach reassures the speaker that their emotions are recognized and important, fostering an atmosphere of trust and openness.

In personal relationships, reflective responses can help partners navigate conflicts by ensuring that each individual's feelings are acknowledged and considered.

Emotional validation is another integral technique in empathetic communication, as it helps diffuse tensions and promotes open, trusting dialogue. Emotional validation involves affirming the speaker's emotions and experiences, regardless of whether the listener agrees with their perspective. It is a way of saying, "I understand why you feel this way," without necessarily endorsing the specific viewpoint or behaviors associated with those feelings. By practicing emotional validation, we create a safe space for authentic communication. This technique encourages individuals to be vulnerable and honest, knowing that their emotions will not be dismissed or belittled. As a result, conversations become more genuine and productive, allowing both parties to address issues collaboratively rather than confrontationally.

Incorporating these techniques into everyday interactions can significantly enhance one's ability to communicate empathetically. For business professionals, mastering these skills can lead to improved networking, client relations, and team dynamics. By fostering empathy in workplace communication, individuals can cultivate environments where everyone feels heard and understood, contributing to higher morale and productivity.

Self-improvement enthusiasts committed to personal growth and emotional intelligence development will find these techniques invaluable in building stronger personal and professional relationships.

Engaging in active listening, posing open-ended questions, offering reflective responses, and providing emotional validation are practical strategies that can be applied across various contexts to enhance interpersonal understanding and connection.

Sales and marketing professionals aiming to refine their communication techniques will also benefit from adopting these practices. Empathetic communication is key to establishing rapport with clients and understanding their needs and desires. By listening actively and responding empathetically, sales professionals can build trust and foster long-term relationships, ultimately improving client engagement and retention.

Empathy's Role in Understanding Perspectives

Cultivating empathy in interactions is vital for enhancing understanding among a diverse range of perspectives. Often, people find themselves in situations where differences lead to misunderstandings and conflicts. Here, perspective-taking plays a crucial role. Perspective-taking involves the conscious effort of stepping into another person's shoes to see things from their vantage point.

It requires more than just acknowledging someone's position; it involves an empathetic shift in thinking. In professional settings, where team dynamics can sometimes be fraught with differing viewpoints, deliberately making space to adopt others' perspectives can mediate tensions and foster more cooperative environments.

Recognizing personal biases is also essential in cultivating empathy. Each person carries their own set of biases, shaped by experiences and cultural backgrounds, which influence how they perceive others. These biases can cloud judgment and hinder the ability to empathize genuinely. By becoming aware of these biases, individuals can begin to challenge them, creating room for empathy to grow.

This self-awareness is a powerful tool for both personal development and improving interpersonal relationships. Being mindful of biases not only enhances empathy but also improves overall communication, enabling individuals to connect on a deeper level with those around them.

Storytelling serves as a remarkable bridge across different perspectives. When we tell stories or listen to them, we invite emotional connections and create pathways for understanding. Stories have a way of transcending barriers, providing insights into emotions and experiences that might otherwise remain foreign. In a business environment, using storytelling can effectively convey messages and establish rapport.

By sharing narratives, whether through presentations or informal conversations, professionals can evoke empathy in their audience, creating resonance and alignment. Storytelling also allows individuals to express their values and experiences creatively, which can enhance team cohesion and client engagement.

Moreover, empathy functions distinctly across various cultures, demanding sensitivity and awareness. Cultural norms shape how empathy is expressed and perceived, meaning what is considered empathetic in one culture may not hold the same weight in another.

For business professionals working in multicultural settings, it's important to understand these nuances. This includes being attuned to non-verbal cues, respecting cultural rituals, and avoiding potential misinterpretations. Sensitivity to cultural differences without making assumptions fosters an inclusive atmosphere where empathy can thrive. In turn, this recognition can lead to more robust international collaborations and partnerships that appreciate and integrate varying worldviews.

Perspective-taking skills can be enhanced through specific strategies. One such method is role-playing, which provides practical experiences of inhabiting another's viewpoint. Whether through structured exercises in training workshops or informal team-building activities, role-playing can deepen empathy and understanding by simulating real-world scenarios.

Similarly, engaging with diverse literature and media offers a window into the lives and mindsets of others. Books and films often provide narratives that enable audiences to explore emotions and contexts that differ from their own. This exposure contributes to a broader comprehension of human experiences, which is invaluable in professions that rely heavily on communication and negotiation, such as sales and marketing.

Active listening further complements perspective-taking by ensuring full engagement with others' points of view. When individuals practice active listening, they prioritize understanding over responding. This commitment to hearing others completely creates an environment where empathy naturally arises.

The act of listening without interruption, coupled with reflective responses that seek clarification, builds trust and openness. Sales professionals, for instance, who excel at active listening can better identify client needs and personalize communications, leading to improved client satisfaction and retention.

In recognizing biases, introspective practices play a crucial role. Reflective thinking encourages individuals to examine their own beliefs and how they impact perceptions of others. Self-reflection prompts questions about why certain biases exist and how they might be altered to facilitate more empathetic interactions. By continuously questioning and exploring personal viewpoints, individuals gradually open themselves to alternative ways of seeing the world, thereby enriching their capacity for empathy.

Encouraging empathy through digital interactions presents unique challenges given the lack of physical presence and non-verbal cues. However, the same principles apply—listening actively, asking open-ended questions, and reflecting on the responses received. Cultivating empathy online calls for a conscious effort to maintain civility and understanding, even when discussions become heated. Recognizing the humanity behind every screen name can help maintain constructive dialogues and foster positive virtual communities.

Overcoming Barriers to Empathy

In the realm of cultivating empathy within interpersonal interactions, one cannot ignore the challenges that can obstruct our ability to connect empathetically with others. Understanding these impediments is crucial for anyone looking to enhance their communication skills, whether in professional settings or personal interactions.

First and foremost, identifying personal barriers is an essential step toward unlocking one's empathetic potential. Stress, a common obstacle, often serves as a significant roadblock. When individuals are overwhelmed by personal stressors, their capacity to empathize diminishes.

The mind tends to focus inward, consumed by personal dilemmas, leaving little room for understanding or considering the emotions of others. Imagine a day at work burdened with deadlines; even the slightest inconvenience from another person can feel like an additional weight. This tunnel vision impairs our ability to respond with compassion and understanding.

Moreover, emotional fatigue can also play a role. Constant exposure to the hardships of others without adequate emotional respite can lead to empathy burnout. It is akin to a nurse who provides care tirelessly, yet over time, begins to feel numb to patient suffering due to relentless emotional demand. Recognizing this pattern is vital because it signals the need for self-care and balanced emotional investment.

Beyond individual struggles, societal norms and digital communication create significant external obstacles to empathy. Social media epitomizes this challenge, where rapid exchanges and superficial interactions often replace meaningful communication. Instead of facilitating connections, digital platforms might inadvertently foster detachment and misunderstanding. As noted in some studies, social media usage can dull the empathic responses of individuals (Mental Health Awareness, 2019).

The depersonalized nature of digital interactions strips away non-verbal cues essential for understanding emotions, thereby hindering genuine engagement. Furthermore, societal pressures that prioritize productivity over relational depth can push empathy to the background, relegating it as an afterthought rather than a central element of human interaction.

Addressing these hurdles requires strategic approaches aimed at rebuilding and strengthening our empathic capabilities. One such strategy is the cultivation of self-compassion. By practicing kindness and understanding toward oneself, individuals build a foundation for extending the same generosity to others.

This approach nurtures emotional resilience, making it easier to step outside personal tribulations and appreciate others' experiences more fully. A business professional navigating challenging negotiation, for instance, will benefit from self-compassion as it allows them to approach discussions with calmness and openness, rather than defensiveness or anxiety.

Improving emotional intelligence is another beneficial strategy. Emotional intelligence encompasses the awareness and management of one's emotions, as well as the ability to discern and influence the emotions of others. Developing this skill set empowers individuals to navigate complex emotional landscapes effectively. For sales professionals aiming to connect deeply and authentically with clients, honing emotional intelligence can transform routine transactions into enriching human interactions, thereby fostering lasting relationships.

Another critical aspect of overcoming barriers to empathetic communication is seeking feedback. Actively requesting insights from colleagues, friends, or mentors can provide clarity on how one's actions are perceived and where improvements are necessary. Feedback acts as a mirror, reflecting areas that may require attention or adjustment. An executive receiving candid feedback about their leadership style, for instance, can use the information to foster a more inclusive and empathetic workplace culture. Constructive insights gained from feedback not only aid personal growth but also enhance organizational dynamics by promoting environments where empathetic behaviors are valued and encouraged.

To successfully overcome barriers to empathy, the above strategies must be tailored according to individual circumstances and contexts. For those entrenched in fast-paced corporate ecosystems, incorporating regular mindfulness practices can help mitigate stress-induced empathic blocks. Business meetings or team collaborations can gain a new dimension when approached with heightened emotional awareness and reduced preoccupations with personal stresses.

Empathy vs. Compassion

Empathy and compassion are often mentioned together, yet they serve distinct roles in our interpersonal interactions. Understanding these differences, as well as their interconnectedness, is crucial for personal and professional growth.

Empathy can be thought of as the bridge that allows us to step into another person's emotional landscape. It involves recognizing and understanding others' emotions, enabling us to connect with their experiences. This cognitive and emotional exercise enriches our perspective, making it easier to build authentic relationships. However, empathy is not just about feeling; it's the starting point for deeper connections. In business settings, empathy helps professionals gauge client moods, anticipate needs, and create tailored solutions, ultimately leading to improved client satisfaction and loyalty.

Compassion, while rooted in empathy, takes a step further by incorporating a call to action. It's characterized by a genuine desire to alleviate suffering. I

n essence, while empathy lets us in on someone else's world, compassion propels us to act on that understanding. For instance, after empathizing with a colleague's stress, compassion would involve offering support, whether through words of encouragement or practical assistance. Compassion thus turns emotions into actions, fostering an environment of care and collaboration.

The interplay between empathy and compassion plays a vital role in promoting social responsibility. Understanding others' emotions through empathy can spark the compassionate drive to address broader societal issues.

For example, when sales and marketing professionals empathize with the challenges faced by consumers, they can design products and messages that not only meet customer needs but also contribute positively to society. This creates a cycle where businesses grow while simultaneously enhancing community welfare.

In the realm of interpersonal communication, empathy and compassion work hand in hand to enhance our interactions. Empathetic listening creates spaces where people feel heard and validated. When combined with compassionate responses, it strengthens trust and fosters open dialogue.

In team dynamics, this duo promotes collaboration and resilience, especially when navigating conflicts or pursuing common goals. By encouraging empathy-first frameworks, businesses can achieve efficient teamwork and innovation.

Moreover, empathy and compassion contribute significantly to emotional intelligence, an essential skill set for effective leadership. Leaders who demonstrate empathy understand their teams better, which in turn cultivates loyalty and motivation. Compassionate leaders then take this insight and implement policies or actions that benefit employee well-being, resulting in increased productivity and job satisfaction.

Empathy's foundational role makes it crucial for the initiation of compassionate actions. By first understanding the depth of someone else's feelings, we lay the groundwork for meaningful interventions.

This progression from empathy to compassion ensures that our actions are informed, appropriate, and impactful.

In customer relations, for instance, empathetic understanding of pain points leads to compassionate service improvements, thereby increasing customer retention and brand advocacy.

Discussing how empathy and compassion enhance communication also highlights their importance in conflict resolution. Empathy allows conflicting parties to appreciate differing perspectives, reducing tensions and paving the way for constructive conversations.

The subsequent application of compassion drives parties towards cooperative solutions, prioritizing mutual respect and shared interests over individual gains. As a result, organizations can foster environments where diverse viewpoints coexist harmoniously, leading to creative problem-solving and heightened innovation.

In sales and marketing, harnessing the power of empathy and compassion can revolutionize client engagement strategies. While empathy helps marketers understand consumer behavior and preferences, compassion enables them to craft campaigns that resonate emotionally and ethically. This approach not only appeals to consumers' emotions but also builds long-lasting relationships anchored in trust and authenticity.

For self-improvement enthusiasts, practicing empathy and compassion enriches personal development journeys. Empathy encourages introspection and mindfulness, prompting individuals to examine their own biases and assumptions. Compassion extends this awareness outward, inspiring actions that nurture relationships and encourage societal contributions. Together, they create pathways for personal growth that emphasize kindness, understanding, and proactive engagement.

Bringing It All Together

Empathy in communication is a multifaceted tool that significantly enriches interpersonal relationships. By understanding and sharing others' emotions, we can build deeper connections and foster genuine understanding. This chapter explored how empathy distinguishes itself from sympathy, emphasizing its role in forming emotional bonds rather than merely acknowledging distress.

Engaging actively through cognitive and emotional empathy allows us to perceive the needs and feelings of those around us, enhancing collaboration and mutual respect. Techniques like active listening and open-ended questioning are practical ways to cultivate empathetic engagement, encouraging richer dialogue and more meaningful connections.

In professional settings, empathy aids business professionals in understanding client needs and promoting better teamwork. Being aware of personal biases and employing storytelling help bridge diverse perspectives, while cultural sensitivity ensures empathy is expressed appropriately across different backgrounds. Though challenges such as stress or digital communication barriers exist, overcoming them through self-compassion and emotional intelligence supports stronger empathic interactions. Ultimately, empathy serves as the foundation for compassionate actions, enriching both personal and professional realms with deeper understanding and authentic relationships.

Chapter 5
Strategizing High-stakes Communication

Strategizing high-stakes communication in professional environments requires a deep understanding of the dynamics at play. Such scenarios often involve intricate exchanges where clarity and confidence are essential for success. Interactions like negotiations, conflicts, or vital presentations present unique challenges that demand strategic thinking. Effective communication is not just about words; it's about adapting to the context, anticipating responses, and managing emotions. This chapter delves into the realm of high-stakes interactions, exploring how professionals can navigate these situations with precision and poise. By mastering the skills needed to handle pressure, individuals can transform daunting conversations into opportunities for growth and success.

The chapter provides an in-depth look at techniques for effective interaction in challenging professional scenarios. It begins with identifying high-stakes situations, helping readers recognize when heightened awareness and communication skills are required. From there, it explores strategies to manage stress and maintain composure during conflicts, including controlled breathing, cognitive reframing, and mindfulness exercises.

The narrative continues by guiding readers on how to adapt language to suit different contexts, emphasizing the importance of aligning tone, selecting appropriate vocabulary, and structuring messages clearly. Furthermore, it discusses assertiveness and clarity, offering practical advice on using "I" statements, setting boundaries, and employing active listening.

The final sections address navigating the consequences of high-stakes communications, empowering readers with insights to anticipate outcomes, reflect on interactions, build resilience, and leverage successes. Through these comprehensive teachings, readers will be equipped with the tools and confidence to engage effectively in high-pressure dialogues, enhancing their professional relationships and advancing their careers.

Identifying High-stakes Situations

Recognizing scenarios that demand heightened communication awareness and skill is crucial for thriving in demanding professional environments. High-stakes situations, such as negotiations, conflicts, or critical presentations, require a nuanced understanding of the communication dynamics at play.

These contexts often involve intricate interpersonal interactions where miscommunication can lead to significant repercussions. Understanding how these scenarios evolve is essential for successful navigation.

Consider a negotiation setting: transactions are not just about exchanging offers; they are about reading between the lines to understand underlying interests. As LeVi (2023) notes, mastering negotiation skills relies heavily on recognizing and managing these subtleties effectively. Recognizing when a conversation transitions into a high-stakes exchange allows professionals to adjust their approach accordingly. The degree of preparation and attentiveness increases dramatically, thus preventing ill-advised decisions that could derail negotiations.

Emotional triggers play a pivotal role in these high-stakes situations. Managing one's emotional responses can significantly impact the outcome of a professional encounter. Research by Brooks (2015) suggests that emotions like anxiety and anger, if left unchecked, can adversely affect communication outcomes.

Being aware of emotional triggers helps individuals modulate their reactions. For instance, feeling anxious before a presentation is common, but channeling that anxiety into positive energy through rehearsal and preparation—suggested by experts—can turn nervousness into enthusiasm, enhancing the delivery and reception of the message.

Similarly, distinguishing urgency levels within high-stakes situations allows for strategic prioritization. Not all issues carry the same weight or demand immediate attention. In crisis management, for example, effective communication begins with identifying what needs immediate action versus what can be addressed subsequently.

Urgency prioritization ensures resources and attention are directed efficiently, reducing stress and improving outcome likelihoods. This strategic decision-making is vital in negotiating deadlines or handling client escalation without compromising overall objectives.

Preparation for unpredictability further enhances adaptability in high-pressure scenarios. Preparing for unforeseen developments prevents being caught off-guard and aids quick adaptation when faced with unexpected challenges. Adaptability requires both mental readiness and flexibility in strategy.

like mergers, acquisitions, or sudden market shifts exemplify unpredictable environments. Building contingency plans as part of preparation helps professionals pivot strategies while maintaining clarity and composure, ensuring conversations remain purposeful and focused, even as conditions change rapidly.

In negotiations particularly, understanding your BATNA (Best Alternative to a Negotiated Agreement), as highlighted by LeVi (2023), equips professionals with leverage, helping them maintain poise and confidence under pressure. When expectations shift, having robust alternatives fosters resilience, allowing negotiators to stay firm on core interests without succumbing to compulsion. Preparation for unpredictability supports maintaining a strategic edge, turning potential setbacks into opportunities for creativity and innovation.

Managing Stress During Conflicts

In the dynamic world of business, professionals often find themselves navigating high-stakes communication scenarios that demand not just verbal proficiency but emotional resilience. At such moments, managing stress effectively can be the key to maintaining composure and ensuring successful interactions.

One of the fundamental strategies to regulate stress during these tense situations is controlled breathing techniques. This approach primarily involves consciously focusing on one's breath to alleviate anxiety and enhance focus.

Consider a scenario where you are about to give a critical presentation to potential clients. Anxiety may creep in, causing your heart rate to spike and your mind to race. Controlled breathing offers a practical solution. By taking slow, deep breaths—inhale for four counts, hold for four counts, and exhale for six counts—you activate your parasympathetic nervous system, which promotes relaxation and helps decrease heart rate. This technique anchors you to the moment, clears mental fog, and primes you for a confident delivery.

Cognitive reframing serves as another powerful tool in stressful communication contexts. It involves altering your perception of a situation to view challenges as opportunities for growth rather than threats. This shift in perspective can transform the way you engage with conflicts.

For instance, instead of seeing a disagreement with a colleague as a hurdle, reframe it as a chance to understand diverse viewpoints and foster collaboration. By adopting this mindset, high-pressure situations become less intimidating and more navigable.

Mindfulness and grounding exercises further complement these strategies by enhancing present-moment awareness. Mindfulness involves paying close attention to your thoughts and sensations without judgment, enabling you to stay centered even when tensions rise.

Grounding exercises, such as focusing on the physical sensations of your feet on the floor or the chair supporting you, help detach from overwhelming emotions and bring your focus back to the present. This anchoring effect allows you to respond thoughtfully rather than react impulsively, improving your overall interaction quality.

Consider a team negotiation meeting that becomes heated. Instead of getting swept away by the rising tension, practicing mindfulness allows you to notice your thoughts and feelings without acting on them immediately. By grounding yourself, you maintain a calm demeanor and a clear head, facilitating more constructive dialogue and better decision-making.

Visualization is another highly effective strategy for managing stress in communication. By picturing positive outcomes before entering a challenging situation, you build psychological readiness and boost confidence.

Visualize walking into the boardroom, interacting calmly and assertively, and concluding with successful outcomes. This technique reduces performance anxiety by mentally rehearsing success, making it feel more attainable in reality. Visualization conditions your mind to anticipate and prepare for desired results, fostering a sense of control and positivity.

These strategies don't just stand alone; they can be woven together to create a comprehensive stress management toolkit. Combining controlled breathing with visualization can set the tone for a grounded and focused approach. Cognitive reframing pairs well with mindfulness to encourage open-mindedness and adaptability in the face of unexpected challenges. Practicing these techniques regularly can transform your approach to high-stakes communication, infusing clarity and composure into every interaction.

For business professionals, these tools are invaluable for enhancing interpersonal communication skills crucial for networking, client engagement, and effective team dynamics. In sales and marketing, mastering stress regulation can lead to more persuasive messaging and stronger client relationships. Meanwhile, self-improvement enthusiasts benefit by integrating emotional intelligence within their personal and professional spheres.

Adapting Language to Suit Contexts

Navigating the waters of high-stakes communication requires a delicate balancing act—adjusting verbal interactions to suit diverse professional contexts is key. Each interaction is an opportunity to build understanding and confidence, ensuring that the intended message is communicated effectively. This subpoint focuses on four primary teachings: aligning tone, selecting appropriate vocabulary, structuring messages clearly, and reading audience reactions.

Tone alignment plays a pivotal role in ensuring that the intention behind any message is accurately perceived. Consider this: when addressing a team after achieving a major milestone, adopting a celebratory tone reinforces collective success and motivation. Conversely, during a performance review, a tone straddling encouragement and constructive criticism promotes productivity and improvement.

Misalignment in tone can lead to misunderstandings or even hostility, potentially derailing the desired outcome. Therefore, it's vital to assess the emotional context of your audience and adjust accordingly. You want your tone to reflect empathy and relevance. Aligning your tone with the expectations of your audience not only aids clarity but also demonstrates emotional intelligence and adaptability.

The words we choose—our vocabulary and jargon—form the backbone of our communication. Tailoring these elements fosters engagement and comprehension. In a technical meeting among engineers, employing industry-specific jargon communicates expertise and efficiency. However, the same jargon might alienate stakeholders unfamiliar with such terminology, necessitating a more universal language approach. T

he goal is always to bridge gaps rather than create them. Understanding the linguistic preferences of your audience ensures that your message resonates, facilitating better outcomes and stronger connections. Reflecting on past interactions can provide insights into which terms and expressions fostered engagement, thus refining future dialogues.

Structuring messages with clarity enhances both retention and professionalism. Whether it's delivering a presentation or writing an email, a well-structured message can ensure all critical points are covered succinctly and logically. Introduce your main idea early, support it with evidence or examples, and conclude with a decisive call to action or summary.

A clear structure acts as a roadmap for the listener, guiding them through your thoughts without losing them along the way. This approach not only maintains professionalism but also aids in establishing your reliability and proficiency on the subject matter. Consistently applying structured communication reinforces your reputation as an effective communicator, enhancing your influence and authority within the workplace.

Lastly, the ability to read the room—understanding audience reactions—is crucial for adapting your language use mid-conversation. This skill involves astutely observing non-verbal cues, such as body language and facial expressions, which can indicate whether your message is being received as intended. For instance, noticing puzzled expressions during a technical explanation might prompt you to simplify your language or provide additional context.

Similarly, enthusiastic nods suggest readiness to proceed to more detailed discussions. Developing this sensitivity allows for immediate adjustments, fostering a dynamic dialogue that remains engaging and productive. Reading audience reactions also involves soliciting direct feedback, either verbally or through quick check-ins, to ensure mutual understanding and alignment.

By adhering to these guidelines—aligning tone, tailoring vocabulary, structuring messages, and reading the room—professionals can enhance their communication efficacy, regardless of the context. These strategies not only improve the exchange of information but also bolster interpersonal relationships, trust, and ultimately, career success.

Through practice and reflection, one can master the art of modifying verbal communication to fit any professional scenario, paving the way for clearer, more confident interactions that resonate with varied audiences.

As you refine these skills, you'll find yourself equipped to handle increasingly complex exchanges with poise and purpose, transcending the challenges inherent in high-stakes communication.

Techniques for Assertiveness and Clarity

In challenging professional scenarios, the importance of clear and assertive communication cannot be overstated. To maintain effective interaction, consider a few techniques that strategically promote assertiveness and clarity while fostering mutual respect and understanding.

Using "I" statements is one simple yet powerful technique. When you use "I" instead of "you," it centers the conversation on your feelings and experiences rather than placing blame or sounding accusatory. For instance, instead of saying, "You always interrupt me," try, "I feel unheard when conversations are interrupted." This subtle shift prevents defensiveness and promotes a more open dialogue.

The technique allows for self-expression in a non-confrontational manner, which can transform potentially tense conversations into productive exchanges. Practice using "I" statements regularly to build comfort with this approach, ultimately enhancing personal and professional relationships.

Equally significant in high-stakes communication is setting clear boundaries. Establishing what is acceptable and what isn't helps communicate your limits and assert your needs effectively. It sends a clear message about which aspects are non-negotiable, reducing misunderstandings.

For example, if a colleague consistently assigns last-minute tasks, a boundary-setting statement might be, "I can manage additional tasks when provided at least three days in advance." By conveying your limits assertively, you respect your own needs while creating an environment where others know your expectations. Over time, these defined boundaries promote healthier working relationships by minimizing conflicts and enhancing overall workflow.

Another indispensable skill is active listening. This form of engaged listening does more than just hear words; it demonstrates empathy and respect, reinforcing assertiveness by valuing the speaker's perspective. Active listening involves several practices: maintaining eye contact, nodding in acknowledgment, and asking clarifying questions to ensure full comprehension.

For example, after someone shares their thoughts, reflecting back with, "What I'm hearing is that you're concerned about the deadline. Could you elaborate?" not only confirms understanding but also touches on the emotional nuances of the conversation. Practicing active listening creates an environment where assertiveness doesn't overshadow mutual respect—each party feels heard and valued, laying the groundwork for constructive discussions. Feedback loops further enhance clarity and reinforce mutual respect in dialogues. This involves exchanging feedback to confirm understanding and agree on actions.

In practice, a feedback loop might look like restating actions decided upon in a meeting, like, "So, to confirm, I will draft the initial proposal by Thursday, and you'll review it by next Tuesday." This ensures that both parties are on the same page, preventing miscommunications and paving the way for collaborative success. Regularly incorporating feedback loops into your communications maintains transparency and trust, driving efficiency and mutual respect across interactions.

Integrating these strategies into your communication toolkit requires dedication. Start small by practicing these skills in everyday conversations with friends or family. As confidence builds, gradually apply them in more challenging professional settings. Remember that communication is an ongoing process, and mastery develops over time through consistent practice.

Consider how each method complements the others, creating a comprehensive approach to assertive communication. "I" statements express personal viewpoints without blaming, setting boundaries communicates non-negotiable elements clearly, active listening shows engagement and respect, and feedback loops ensure aligned understanding.

Embracing this holistic framework not only elevates individual dialogues but also contributes to a culture of transparent, respectful communication within teams and organizations.

Navigating Consequences of High-stakes Communication

In high-stakes professional interactions, understanding and addressing potential consequences is crucial for effective communication. Such insights allow individuals to navigate these discussions with strategic foresight and the ability to manage outcomes, whether they align with expectations or not. Anticipating potential outcomes is a key component of strategic preparation. Before entering a high-stakes conversation, it is beneficial to envisage various scenarios that might unfold. Consider the best-case, worst-case, and most likely outcomes. This mental exercise equips you to respond more dynamically during the actual interaction, as you will have already contemplated critical responses or solutions.

For example, when preparing for a negotiation, anticipate objections and prepare counterarguments. Additionally, having contingency plans in place can alleviate stress, allowing a more focused approach during dialogues.

Once the interaction has concluded, managing post-interaction reflections becomes vital. Reflecting on what transpired helps identify both the successes and areas needing improvement. This process should be systematic; consider keeping a journal or notes on the interaction to aid in detailed retrospection.

Analyzing your performance helps uncover patterns and habits—both positive and negative—that recur during your high-stakes communications. By identifying these patterns, you can cultivate better strategies for future interactions. For instance, if you notice frequent miscommunication regarding project details, you might work on clarifying language or checking understanding more often during conversations.

Developing resilience is another essential aspect of handling undesired results constructively. In high-pressure situations, outcomes may not always favor one's intentions. Instead of viewing these outcomes as failures, consider them learning opportunities.

Resilience involves acknowledging setbacks, analyzing their causes, and recalibrating your approach. It might involve seeking feedback from colleagues or mentors who participated in or witnessed the interaction. Such feedback can provide outside perspectives that you might have overlooked.

Moreover, using setbacks to hone one's skills contributes to personal growth and enhances emotional intelligence over time. This adaptability ensures that even when discussions don't go as planned, subsequent efforts are informed by prior experiences and insights, transforming past setbacks into future strengths.

Lastly, leveraging successful engagements is pivotal in strengthening future communication strategies. Whenever you achieve favorable outcomes, take time to dissect which elements of your approach yielded positive results. Was it your preparation, the manner of delivery, or perhaps the timing?

Understanding these factors allows you to replicate and build upon successful techniques in future interactions. Share these strategies within your professional network to receive input and further refinements.

By doing so, you create a feedback loop that not only acknowledges your accomplishments but also positions you as a resourceful communicator among peers. Cumulatively, these strategies lead to a repertoire of communication tactics—each tailored from real-world experiences—which enhance your confidence and efficacy in future high-stakes situations.

In summary, a nuanced understanding of potential consequences in high-stakes communication offers pathways for preparedness and reflection. Through anticipation, reflection, resilience, and leveraging success, professionals can refine their communication skills. This iterative process transforms each interaction into an opportunity for growth, equipping individuals to handle complex scenarios with increased confidence and clarity.

Bringing It All Together

In this chapter, we've explored the intricacies of handling high-stakes professional interactions with confidence and clarity. Recognizing such scenarios, whether in negotiations, conflicts, or critical presentations, requires an acute awareness of communication dynamics. We've discussed how understanding emotional triggers and employing strategies like controlled breathing, cognitive reframing, and mindfulness helps navigate these challenging situations effectively.

Moreover, adapting language to various contexts by aligning tone, selecting appropriate vocabulary, and structuring messages clearly ensures that your message resonates well with diverse audiences. The emphasis on reading audience reactions further enhances adaptability, allowing for smoother interactions that foster trust and understanding.

We also delved into techniques for assertiveness and clarity, highlighting the importance of "I" statements, setting boundaries, active listening, and utilizing feedback loops. These tools collectively promote open dialogue and mutual respect, transforming high-stakes exchanges into opportunities for collaboration and growth. Navigating potential consequences involves strategic preparation, reflection on experiences, and resilience in face of setbacks.

By leveraging past successes and learning from challenges, professionals can refine their approaches, turning each interaction into a stepping stone for enhanced communication skills. This comprehensive toolkit is invaluable for business and sales professionals alike, offering pathways to elevate career trajectories and strengthen personal relationships through improved interpersonal communication.

Chapter 6

Reading Between the Lines

Extracting core meanings from verbal exchanges and indirect communications is a vital competency in navigating complex conversational landscapes. The ability to read between the lines enhances our understanding of what lies beneath the surface of words, giving us insight into the nuances and emotions that might not be immediately apparent. This chapter delves into how language can convey deeper intentions and messages through tone, choice of words, and context beyond their literal meaning. By developing this skill, individuals can improve their effectiveness in both personal and professional interactions.

This chapter explores various strategies to help readers master the art of discerning subtext in conversations. It covers practical exercises designed to sharpen interpretative abilities, allowing one to detect underlying messages and respond appropriately. By doing so, business professionals will find methods to enhance their interpersonal communication skills, aiding in networking and team dynamics.

Meanwhile, self-improvement enthusiasts will discover techniques to bolster emotional intelligence, and sales and marketing professionals will learn how to refine their messaging for better client engagement and retention. Whether through analytical exercises or role-playing scenarios, these approaches offer valuable insights into recognizing not just spoken words but also the underlying sentiments they may carry.

Identifying Insinuations and Subtext

Recognizing and interpreting subtext in conversations is an essential skill for navigating both professional and personal interactions. Subtext involves understanding what isn't explicitly said but is implied through tone, context, and choice of words. By mastering the art of reading between the lines, you can uncover hidden meanings behind spoken words and improve your communication effectiveness.

Language frequently carries more than its literal meaning, adding layers of complexity to our interactions. When someone says, "That's interesting," they might genuinely find the conversation engaging, or they could be dismissing it politely. The true intention often depends on subtle cues that carry additional weight beyond the surface of the words used. Understanding these nuances requires an awareness of how language is utilized to convey deeper emotions and intentions that are not immediately apparent.

Real-life scenarios further illustrate how simple phrases can imply deeper meanings like criticism or appreciation. Consider a workplace meeting where a manager tells an employee, "You've really outdone yourself this time." Depending on prior exchanges, this comment could indicate genuine praise for exceptional work or sarcastically suggest that the employee has made a significant error. Recognizing subtext helps in discerning these differences and responding appropriately, thereby fostering healthier communication dynamics.

One effective way to hone these interpretative skills is through practical exercises. Analytical exercises involving media—such as movies, TV shows, or news broadcasts—can provide valuable insight into the subtleties of language. Watching interactions unfold and noting instances of sarcasm, irony, or unspoken tension sharpens one's ability to detect insincerities and genuine exchanges.

Role-playing exercises also offer hands-on experience by simulating various conversational contexts, allowing individuals to practice identifying underlying messages. These activities engage participants in deciphering the real intent behind dialogues, equipping them with strategies to read between the lines in everyday situations.

Additionally, understanding the role of tone and situational context is crucial in transforming the implication of statements. A question posed with an inquisitive tone during a casual lunch may feel friendly and engaging, but the same question asked sternly in a formal meeting might be perceived as challenging or accusatory. Context shapes the interaction, influencing how the message is received. Paying attention to where and how words are delivered enhances comprehension, paving the way for more meaningful dialogue.

The importance of subtext extends to various aspects of life, from building professional relationships to nurturing personal connections. In a business environment, recognizing subtext can lead to improved networking abilities and client interactions. It helps professionals navigate complex team dynamics by addressing concerns that are subtly voiced rather than directly stated. For self-improvement enthusiasts, developing the ability to interpret subtext contributes to heightened emotional intelligence, ultimately resulting in better interpersonal skills and stronger relationships.

For sales and marketing professionals, understanding subtext is critical for refining communication techniques. When engaging clients, the ability to discern hesitation or excitement beneath spoken words allows for more persuasive messaging. This sensitivity to nuanced language aids in crafting responses that align with the client's true feelings, thus enhancing engagement and fostering long-term relationships.

Contextual Analysis of Dialogue

Understanding context is crucial for interpreting conversations meaningfully. Whether in business or personal interactions, the subtleties of conversation are often shaped by the context they're set in. This means that a statement, a gesture, or even silence can carry different meanings depending on the surrounding circumstances.

For instance, consider humor. A joke shared among close friends might be received with laughter and understanding. However, the same joke told in a professional meeting could result in awkwardness or misinterpretation. Here, the context—the level of familiarity and the setting—changes the reception and interpretation drastically.

Recognizing these variations helps prevent miscommunications and fosters more effective dialogues.

Shared experiences between participants add another layer to conversational context. Imagine two colleagues who have worked together on numerous projects; their interactions are likely peppered with references to past events and mutual understandings. These shared histories create an implicit backdrop that colors current exchanges.

Without acknowledging this shared past, new participants in the conversation might find themselves lost or misunderstanding the content. Therefore, reflecting on previous interactions and using them as reference points can enhance clarity and cohesion in ongoing communications.

Cultural backgrounds significantly influence how we interpret conversations. Cultural norms dictate what is considered polite or rude, humorous or offensive. They shape verbal and non-verbal communication styles, from body language to the tone of voice used.

The concept of high-context cultures versus low-context cultures provides insight into these differences. High-context cultures, like those in Asia and Latin America, rely heavily on unspoken cues and prior knowledge of relationships. In contrast, low-context cultures, such as the United States and Northern Europe, prioritize explicit verbal communication with less reliance on situational context.

This cultural context can lead to misunderstandings if not acknowledged. For example, in a multicultural team, a manager's direct feedback may be appreciated by employees from low-context cultures but perceived as harsh by those from high-context cultures. This highlights the necessity of cultural awareness in communication. By recognizing and adapting to these cultural influences, one can navigate conversations more effectively, fostering inclusion and reducing potential conflicts.

Proactively considering context before responding in any interaction is an invaluable skill. It allows for measured, thoughtful engagement rather than reactive, potentially misguided responses.

Practical scenarios abound: suppose you're at a networking event where a colleague brings up an industry change that you have different views on. Instead of jumping into a rebuttal, pausing to assess the colleague's perspective and the event's atmosphere can guide a more productive discussion.

Similarly, during negotiations, observing the other party's demeanor and the situation's formality can offer clues about their stance and priorities. Engaging with context in mind encourages a deeper understanding of others' positions and motivations, ultimately leading to more successful communication outcomes.

To strengthen this skill, practice analyzing interactions with context in mind. Begin with everyday situations: a family dinner, a team meeting, or a casual chat with a neighbor.

Pay attention to the various elements at play—relationships, settings, and cultural nuances—and observe how they shape the direction and meaning of the conversation. Reflect on your interpretations and responses, adjusting them as needed based on these insights.

Engaging in role-playing exercises can further refine this ability. By stepping into diverse contexts intentionally and evaluating responses, one gains practical experience in managing a range of communicative environments. Consider scenarios where context dramatically shifts meaning—a solemn meeting compared to a casual coffee break—and practice shifting your communication style accordingly.

Recognizing Signs of Miscommunication

Detecting early signs of miscommunication is a critical skill in both personal and professional interactions. When we engage in conversations, it's easy to assume that our message is understood as intended. However, verbal indicators such as questions expressing confusion or responses that don't align with the topic suggest a disconnect. These signals are often the first hint that our communication has not been as clear as we believed.

Consider a scenario in a business meeting where a team member repeatedly asks for clarification on points you thought were evident. This indicates a potential misunderstanding. Such verbal cues prompt us to revisit our explanations and ensure our points are articulated more clearly using simpler language or additional examples.

Similarly, non-verbal cues play an integral role in conveying meaning. Often, these cues can reveal misunderstandings separate from verbal exchanges. Body language, like crossed arms or a lack of eye contact, might imply discomfort or disagreement. Facial expressions such as furrowing brows or pursed lips can indicate confusion or skepticism about what is being communicated. In group settings, observing these non-verbal signals provides an opportunity to address any unease directly, ensuring all participants remain on the same page.

In seeking to correct miscommunication, feedback serves as a vital tool. Feedback doesn't merely clarify messages; it fosters a two-way interaction that enhances understanding.

When engaged in discussions, actively soliciting feedback ensures that both parties are interpreting the conversation correctly. Simple questions like "Does that make sense?" or "How would you proceed based on this information?" help gauge the receiver's understanding and invite their input.

Providing feedback is equally important. Constructive feedback encourages openness and allows individuals to adjust their approach if needed. A culture of open dialogue and feedback enables teams to address potential miscommunications swiftly, preventing them from escalating into larger issues.

Corrective measures involve approaching conversations with an open mind and willingness to adapt as necessary. Entering discussions without preconceived notions helps prevent bias from affecting how messages are delivered or received. Miscommunication often arises when parties cling too strongly to predetermined ideas, so remaining flexible and receptive to new information is crucial.

When confronted with unexpected responses or body language that suggests misunderstanding, taking a step back and considering alternative explanations or perspectives can illuminate the root cause of the miscommunication. An open-minded approach encourages individuals to listen more attentively and respond thoughtfully, bridging the gap between differing viewpoints.

Moreover, adopting strategies like summarizing key points, asking open-ended questions, and restating others' ideas in your own words further facilitate better understanding. These techniques ensure alignment between what is said and how it is perceived while promoting active listening.

It's also important to acknowledge the influence of noise, distractions, and emotional barriers on effective communication. Physical noise or mental distractions during exchanges can lead to missed nuances or incomplete comprehension.

Eliminating external disturbances during crucial dialogues by choosing quieter environments or managing one's internal state through mindfulness practices can significantly reduce such risks.

Emotionally charged situations often distort perceptions, leading to defensive or hostile reactions. Cultivating emotional intelligence empowers individuals to recognize their emotions and manage them constructively within communications, fostering environments where clarity prevails over chaos. Cultural differences, though enriching workplaces, may pose challenges too. Diverse backgrounds can mean different interpretations rooted in cultural norms. Being mindful of these differences and encouraging inclusivity by acknowledging various cultural contexts enriches dialogues and minimizes misunderstanding.

While digital platforms offer convenience in remote and hybrid work setups, they also strip away non-verbal cues that facilitate natural understanding. Asynchronous communication, like emails or text messages, lacks immediacy and context, potentially creating confusion. Being explicit in written communications, avoiding ambiguous language, and using visual aids like emojis or bullet points where necessary enhances clarity.

Finally, recognizing the distinction between miscommunication, which involves failures in delivering the intended message, and misunderstanding, where correct messages are interpreted incorrectly, addresses the issue more effectively. By focusing efforts on refining expression and reception, miscommunications are less likely to transform into persistent misunderstandings.

Understanding Cultural Influences on Meaning

In the realm of communication, cultural backgrounds serve as a powerful lens through which individuals interpret and engage with the world around them. These cultural norms and expectations significantly shape communication styles, affecting not only what is said but also how it is perceived by others. This dynamic becomes particularly evident when people from different cultural backgrounds interact, each bringing their own set of assumptions and expectations to the conversation.

Cultural norms often dictate the nature of verbal exchanges. For instance, in high-context cultures, such as Japan or China, communication tends to rely heavily on implicit messages and contextual cues. Here, the words spoken are just a fraction of the overall message, while tone, context, and non-verbal signals carry substantial weight.

In contrast, low-context cultures like the United States or Germany prioritize directness and clarity. The emphasis here is on explicit communication, where the spoken word conveys the majority of the intended message (Tidwell, 2016).

These differences can lead to misunderstandings if not accounted for. A Japanese business partner might interpret an American colleague's forthrightness as brusque or rude, while the American might find the Japanese partner's indirectness confusing. Understanding these distinctions is vital for effective intercultural communication and can aid in avoiding misinterpretations that may arise from differing cultural expectations.

Beyond verbal communication, non-verbal gestures vary significantly across cultures and can profoundly impact communication clarity.

Actions such as eye contact, handshakes, or personal space preferences all bear cultural significance. In some Western cultures, maintaining steady eye contact is seen as a sign of confidence and honesty.

However, in certain Asian and Middle Eastern cultures, prolonged eye contact might be perceived as confrontational or disrespectful. Similarly, a firm handshake is standard in many countries, conveying professionalism, while in others, such physical contact might be considered too assertive or even intrusive (tsakelson@ufl.edu, 2023).

To navigate these complexities, adapting communication strategies based on cultural insights is crucial. Professionals who tailor their approach by considering cultural backgrounds foster better dialogue and collaboration.

One effective strategy is to engage in active listening, which involves paying close attention not just to words but also to tone, silence, and body language. By doing so, communicators can glean additional information about the speaker's intentions and the cultural context of their message.

Moreover, being open to feedback and displaying a willingness to adjust one's communication style is indispensable. Encouraging cross-cultural training in workplaces can also help employees develop these skills. Such training can include role-playing scenarios where participants practice adjusting their non-verbal cues or verbal communication to align better with those from different cultural backgrounds.

Practical exercises for identifying biases and analyzing scenarios can be instrumental in avoiding cultural misalignments that might lead to conflict.

One useful exercise is to reflect on past interactions, particularly those that were challenging, and evaluate them through a cultural lens. This practice helps individuals identify unconscious biases that might have influenced their interpretation or behavior.

Analyzing case studies involving cross-cultural communication challenges can further enhance understanding and prepare individuals for future encounters.For example, consider a scenario where a team of international colleagues collaborates on a project.

By examining the dynamics through cultural dimensions—such as individualism versus collectivism or high-context versus low-context communication—team members can become more aware of how each participant's cultural background influences their communication style. Addressing these differences upfront allows for smoother interactions and reduces potential friction.

Additionally, group discussions following such exercises offer valuable opportunities for sharing insights and personal experiences, fostering empathy and a deeper appreciation for diverse perspectives. These discussions should emphasize that no single communication style is superior; instead, they highlight the importance of adaptability and mutual respect in achieving effective communication.

The proverb "actions speak louder than words" aptly underscores the significance of non-verbal communication in intercultural settings. Gestures, facial expressions, posture, and other forms of body language often carry meanings that transcend verbal messages. Being mindful of these elements, particularly in an intercultural context, enhances understanding and minimizes the risk of misunderstandings.

Practical Application of Reading Between the Lines

Unlocking the potential to interpret nuanced communication is a journey that involves practical techniques and reflective exercises. In our fast-paced environments, conversations flow quickly, often leaving little room for careful interpretation.

One effective approach to enhance understanding is through retrospective analysis of past interactions. By reflecting on previous conversations, individuals can identify moments where they overlooked subtleties or indirect messages. This practice not only sharpens one's awareness but also builds a repository of experiences from which to draw insights in future exchanges.

A structured exercise to facilitate this reflection involves revisiting past dialogues and pinpointing specific instances where insinuations may have been missed.

For example, consider a project meeting where a colleague's hesitant tone might have hinted at underlying concerns. Reflecting on such scenarios helps in recognizing patterns in human behavior and linguistic cues, allowing for more informed responses in subsequent interactions. This iterative process of learning and applying these insights creates a cycle of continuous improvement in communication skills.

Adapting communication style according to context is another pivotal skill for decoding complex messages. This entails adjusting one's tone, formality, and directness based on the environment and audience. For instance, a conversation with senior executives requires a different approach compared to casual chats with team members.

Recognizing these distinctions enables professionals to tailor their communication, thereby increasing the effectiveness of their message delivery. Understanding when to be succinct or when to elaborate further can significantly impact the clarity and reception of the intended message.

Practical exercises that can assist in honing this skill include role-playing scenarios with varying degrees of formality and expected outcomes.

Participants can simulate situations like delivering constructive feedback to a peer versus addressing a misunderstanding with a client. Through these activities, individuals gain firsthand experience in employing different communication strategies tailored to specific contexts. Role play serves as a safe space to experiment with diverse approaches, fostering adaptability and enhancing confidence in real-world situations.

Moreover, hands-on experience in recognizing subtext and implicit messages can be gained through targeted role-play activities. These exercises not only cultivate the ability to discern underlying messages but also offer insight into how others perceive and interpret communication cues.

By engaging in simulated dialogues, individuals can practice identifying non-verbal signals such as body language and facial expressions, which often accompany spoken words and contribute significantly to the full meaning of a conversation.

Applying these learned skills to everyday interactions is essential for sustained progress in understanding nuanced communication. Practical tips for doing so include consciously pausing during conversations to evaluate the multi-layered meanings behind words and gestures. Embracing a mindset of active inquiry encourages clarification of ambiguous statements and promotes mutual understanding.

By continually seeking to refine one's ability to decode complexities in communication, professionals can nurture stronger relationships and foster an environment of openness and collaboration.

Real-life application of these skills could involve conducting a self-assessment after crucial business meetings or personal discussions. Identifying what worked well and areas for improvement helps in crafting a personalized strategy for tackling future communication challenges. Constant engagement in reflective practices aligns with the notion of lifelong learning, wherein each interaction becomes an opportunity to test and expand one's communication prowess.

The pursuit of improved interpretative communication techniques benefits various audiences, whether business professionals aiming for better networking results or self-improvement enthusiasts eager to develop emotional intelligence.

It equips individuals with the tools necessary to navigate both professional settings and personal interactions with greater dexterity and insight. Whether it is the intricacies involved in negotiating client contracts or nurturing trusted team dynamics, mastering these skills unlocks doors to more meaningful and effective exchanges.

Bringing It All Together

In this chapter, we delved into the nuanced art of recognizing insinuations and subtext in communication. By understanding what lies beneath the surface of verbal exchanges, readers can enhance their interaction skills across various settings. We explored how language often carries meanings beyond its literal interpretations and how subtleties like tone and context shape our conversations.

Real-life scenarios illustrated how simple phrases could convey deeper intentions, such as sarcasm or praise, depending on previous interactions and situational contexts. We also highlighted the significance of cultural influences on communication styles, emphasizing the need for awareness and adaptability to prevent misunderstandings and foster inclusivity.

Additionally, the chapter offered practical strategies for honing the ability to read between the lines, such as engaging in media analysis and role-playing exercises. These techniques provide hands-on experience, allowing individuals to practice identifying underlying messages in diverse conversations.

By refining these interpretative skills, business professionals, self-improvement enthusiasts, and sales and marketing specialists alike can better navigate interpersonal dynamics. Through continuous reflection and adaptation based on contextual cues and cultural insights, readers are equipped to build stronger relationships, communicate more effectively, and achieve desired outcomes in their professional and personal lives.

Chapter 7

Adapting Communication Styles for Success

Adapting communication styles is a matter of understanding the diverse landscapes in which interactions occur. Communication plays a pivotal role in both personal and professional relationships, influencing how our messages are perceived and understood. Each environment and audience present unique challenges and opportunities that necessitate careful consideration of how we convey our thoughts. Understanding these nuances can transform ordinary exchanges into pathways for mutual understanding and success. By tailoring our communication styles to fit different contexts, we enhance clarity and foster stronger connections, making them more meaningful and productive.

This chapter delves into the intricacies of adapting communication styles, exploring how to align messaging with varied audiences and environments. It begins by examining the fundamental importance of adjusting one's approach to suit different settings, whether in formal meetings or casual conversations.

Readers will find strategies for recognizing the subtleties of each interaction, including the significance of cultural awareness and non-verbal cues. Additionally, this chapter provides insights into the methods and techniques professionals can use to hone their adaptability skills.

Feedback mechanisms, such as peer reviews and self-assessments, play a crucial role, offering valuable perspectives on what resonates with an audience. Through practical guidelines and illustrative scenarios, the chapter equips individuals with the tools needed to navigate the complexities of modern communication, ultimately empowering them to achieve greater success in their personal and professional endeavors.

Understanding Personal Communication Styles

Understanding one's communication style is the first crucial step toward more effective interactions in both personal and professional settings. Each person has a dominant communication style that broadly falls into three categories: assertive, passive, and aggressive. Recognizing which category, you primarily operate within can offer significant insights into how you interact with others and how they perceive you.

Assertive communicators tend to express their thoughts, feelings, and desires openly and respectfully. They stand up for themselves while respecting the rights of others, making them excellent collaborators who facilitate open dialogue and mutual respect. On the other hand, passive communicators often avoid expressing their own needs or desires, sometimes leading to misunderstandings or unmet expectations. Meanwhile, aggressive communicators may dominate discussions, often at the expense of others' perspectives, potentially creating tension.

Self-awareness is essential for identifying your dominant communication style. It plays an integral role in personal reflection, offering a deeper understanding of how you relate to others and manage interactions. Self-awareness does not merely stop at recognizing your communication style; it extends to understanding the origins of this style. For instance, cultural norms, upbringing, and past experiences can all shape how we communicate. By reflecting on these influences, individuals gain a clearer picture of their communication tendencies.

Recognizing the strengths and weaknesses associated with each style is another layer of understanding necessary for improvement. Assertive communicators often build strong relationships based on trust and clarity.

However, they must guard against becoming overly dominant in situations requiring collective input. Passive communicators may excel in listening and observing but might need to work on asserting their opinions more frequently to ensure their needs are met. Aggressive communicators, while efficient in reaching goals quickly, may benefit from focusing on empathy and understanding to foster better collaboration.

Awareness of these characteristics allows individuals to strategically enhance their relationship-building skills. For example, if you identify as a passive communicator, you can work on strategies for speaking up in meetings or setting boundaries in conversations. Conversely, if you are naturally aggressive, adopting practices such as active listening and asking for feedback can improve how others perceive and respond to you.

To aid in this identification process, self-assessment tools like quizzes provide immediate insights into one's communication style. These quizzes typically consist of a series of questions designed to evaluate how you handle different communication scenarios, revealing underlying patterns and preferences. (Inabo, 2021). Although these quizzes give a useful snapshot of one's communication profile, they should be viewed as complementary to ongoing self-reflection and development rather than definitive answers.

For those committed to developing a more versatile communication skill set, embracing a flexible mindset is essential. While each individual has preferred ways of communicating, successful interactions often require adapting styles to better fit the context and audience. This flexibility not only enhances communication efficacy but also signals a high level of emotional intelligence (Murphy, 2017).

One practical guideline for cultivating a flexible mindset is to practice observing nonverbal cues during interactions. Paying attention to body language, facial expressions, and tone can reveal much about others' communication preferences and mood. This mindfulness allows for real-time adjustments, ensuring that interactions remain positive and productive.

Additionally, engaging in role-playing exercises or simulations can prepare individuals for varying communication contexts, helping them practice different styles. Such exercises enhance adaptability by providing hands-on experience in switching between styles based on specific situational demands. Regular feedback from peers or mentors during these sessions can further refine one's ability to adjust communication tactics, ultimately contributing to more sophisticated interpersonal skills.

Self-assessment tools deserve special mention as effective resources for personal growth in communication. Beyond quizzes, these tools include reflective journaling, peer assessments, and engaging in workshops that focus on communication skill-building.

Reflective journaling provides a space for individuals to document their communication experiences, analyze outcomes, and track progress over time. Meanwhile, peer assessments bring external perspectives, offering valuable insights into how others perceive your communication approach.

Workshops dedicated to enhancing communication skills create opportunities for direct interaction and feedback. Participants in these sessions benefit from group dynamics, practicing in real-life scenarios, and receiving constructive criticism in a supportive environment. Commitment to these methods fosters continuous improvement, elevating one's communication abilities to new heights.

Adapting Styles Across Different Settings

In today's fast-paced and interconnected world, adapting communication styles is no longer just useful but essential for success. Recognizing contextual differences in communication helps ensure that our messages are both clear and relevant to the audience. Whether it's a formal board meeting or an informal chat with colleagues over lunch, understanding the nuances of each setting allows professionals to tailor their communication effectively.

One of the most effective ways of recognizing these differences is by analyzing the environment in which communication takes place. For instance, the atmosphere of a creative brainstorming session might encourage open-ended questions and collaborative dialogue, whereas a financial review meeting could require concise and factual reporting.

To help navigate these diverse environments, one can apply guidelines like assessing the formality of the setting and noting any specific cultural tendencies within the group. Identifying these contextual elements enhances message clarity and avoids potential miscommunication.

Adapting communication in real-time poses a unique challenge that requires agility and attentiveness. Strategies such as mirroring and active listening become invaluable tools in such instances.

Mirroring involves subtly imitating the body language, vocal tone, or speech patterns of your conversational partner to build rapport and convey empathy. When done naturally, it signals a willingness to establish connection and understanding.

Active listening, on the other hand, ensures that the communicator fully understands the other party's perspective before responding. This technique emphasizes genuine listening rather than merely hearing words being spoken.

By focusing on the speaker and maintaining an open mind, individuals can adapt their responses to be more attuned and relevant, creating more meaningful interactions. The use of silence at appropriate times can further enhance this process by providing space for reflection and thought, encouraging more deliberate and intentional communication.

Cultural awareness is another vital aspect when adjusting communication styles to fit specific environments. In our increasingly globalized business landscape, respecting cultural norms is crucial to preventing misunderstandings and fostering inclusive interactions. Every culture has distinct communication styles, from variations in eye contact and gestures to differing interpretations of punctuality and formality.

An example can be found in business meetings across different cultures: while Western settings may value directness and efficiency, Eastern contexts might prioritize harmony and indirect communication. Understanding these subtleties enables professionals to approach cross-cultural exchanges with sensitivity and respect, ultimately enhancing mutual comprehension and collaboration.

As (Cromarty, 2021) highlights, cultural adaptability not only helps overcome challenges but also strengthens teamwork and contributes to a more productive workplace.

Feedback mechanisms are indispensable for evaluating the effectiveness of adapted communication strategies. Constructive feedback plays a crucial role in identifying what works and what doesn't, enabling individuals to refine their approach continually.

Implementing a feedback loop that involves peers, supervisors, or even clients can provide insights into areas that need improvement, leading to better alignment with the intended audience.

Assessing the impact of communication styles through feedback also fosters accountability, encouraging communicators to remain committed to growth and development.

It's beneficial to create opportunities for two-way feedback in team settings, allowing for open discussions about communication preferences and expectations.

Moreover, incorporating regular self-assessments can help track progress and identify patterns that may require adjustment. By valuing feedback as a tool for enhancement, professionals can fine-tune their messaging techniques for maximum impact.

Adaptation doesn't stop at acknowledging cultural norms or real-time adjustments; it's an ongoing journey of learning and evolving. Individuals must be willing to embrace change and view adaptation as an integral part of their professional toolkit. This mindset shift empowers them to face diverse situations with confidence and competence, paving the path for successful interactions across various contexts.

Ultimately, mastering the art of communication adaptation means embracing flexibility and being open to new perspectives. As professionals grow more adept at tailoring their communication styles to suit different environments, they not only improve their interpersonal skills but also build stronger relationships with colleagues, clients, and stakeholders alike.

Utilizing Feedback for Adaptation

In the intricate dance of communication, feedback serves as both a mirror and a map—reflecting areas for improvement and guiding the path to success. Recognizing the various types of feedback is fundamental to refining one's communication style, whether in business dealings, personal growth, or sales strategies.

Understanding that feedback can take many forms is crucial. Constructive feedback, for instance, highlights areas that may be confusing or need clarification. It helps communicators refine their messages and enhance clarity, such as when a listener asks for a point to be re-explained for better understanding (Bernard, 2023).

Positive feedback, on the other hand, affirms successful communication practices and encourages the continuation of beneficial behaviors. For example, a listener might confirm agreement with the speaker's points, offering reassurance and support. Nonverbal cues also play a significant role, where gestures like nodding or maintaining eye contact signal engagement and comprehension. By recognizing these varied signals, individuals can identify specific areas needing refinement, tailoring their communication styles accordingly.

Creating a continuous feedback loop not only fosters accountability but also promotes an environment conducive to growth. In the realm of professional development, this loop acts as a catalyst for ongoing refinement and mastery of communication skills. Feedback should be gathered through various channels, such as one-on-one conversations, team meetings, or anonymous surveys, ensuring accessibility for all participants.

Implementing tools that facilitate instant feedback can be particularly effective in fast-paced environments, providing immediate insights that can be acted upon quickly. This continuous exchange transforms feedback from a sporadic occurrence into a habitual practice, embedding it within the organizational culture. Guidelines for establishing a feedback loop include setting clear objectives for feedback sessions, such as identifying specific communication goals. Encourage open dialogue by creating a safe space where individuals feel comfortable sharing honest feedback without fear of repercussions.

Regular check-ins, like weekly meetings or post-project reviews, can help maintain momentum and ensure feedback remains relevant and actionable. Finally, closing the loop by communicating changes made based on feedback reinforces its importance and demonstrates responsiveness, encouraging further participation (Fermin, 2023).

Developing constructive responses to feedback is another essential step in this process. Effective communication requires adapting to the input received, rather than simply reacting to it. When given feedback, especially if it is critical, it's important to acknowledge the comments without becoming defensive. Responding constructively might involve paraphrasing the feedback to ensure understanding and then discussing possible adjustments to improve communication outcomes. This approach not only addresses the immediate feedback but also sets a foundation for continual improvement.

Practical techniques for integrating feedback include actively seeking clarification when initial feedback seems vague or broad. Asking questions such as "How can I improve this specific area?" or "What alternative approach would you suggest?" turns feedback into a dialogue, fostering collaborative problem-solving.

Using "I" statements when responding can personalize the interaction, making it less confrontational and more focused on mutual goals. For instance, saying "I understand your concerns about my presentation pace; I'll work on slowing down to ensure clarity" illustrates a willingness to adapt and grow.

Tracking progress through self and peer evaluations is crucial in measuring improvements in communication. Self-assessments allow individuals to reflect on their communication experiences, identifying patterns of success and areas needing enhancement.

By comparing these reflections with peer evaluations, communicators gain a comprehensive view of their strengths and weaknesses, enabling targeted development.

To implement this effectively, consider establishing periodic evaluation milestones to assess progress consistently over time. Encourage peers to provide specific examples during evaluations, as detailed feedback contributes to more precise adjustments.

Utilizing metrics or benchmarks can also help quantify improvements, making the growth journey visible. Additionally, celebrating successes, no matter how small, can motivate continuous efforts toward refining communication skills.

In conclusion, feedback plays a pivotal role in shaping effective communication. By recognizing diverse feedback types, creating a structured feedback loop, developing constructive responses, and regularly tracking progress, individuals and organizations can significantly enhance their communication styles. This not only leads to improved interpersonal interactions but also fosters environments where growth, collaboration, and success thrive. The commitment to embracing feedback as a tool for development ultimately paves the way for more meaningful connections and better overall outcomes in professional and personal spheres.

Effectively Transitioning Between Styles

A key strategy for effective communication is seamlessly transitioning between different styles to resonate with diverse audiences and environments. To facilitate this adaptation, one must first understand specific scenarios where such transitions are not just beneficial but necessary for effective messaging.

For instance, in a cross-cultural business meeting, being able to switch from an assertive to a more nuanced style can bridge cultural gaps and foster mutual understanding.

Similarly, engaging with various stakeholders in a corporate setting might require toggling between a formal style for upper management and a more relaxed tone for peers or subordinates. Recognizing the contexts that demand style shifts is critical to maintaining clarity and achieving communication goals.

Once these scenarios are identified, employing techniques like pausing and pacing transitions becomes indispensable. Pausing during conversations allows time to assess the audience's reactions and adjust the communication style accordingly.

This deliberate pause can also provide a moment to consider the next best approach before proceeding, ensuring the message remains relevant and engaging.

Meanwhile, pacing involves controlling the speed of speech to match the listener's comfort level. Speaking too quickly can overwhelm an audience, while a slower pace might cause loss of interest. By modulating both the speed and rhythm of their delivery, communicators can maintain attention and ensure their message lands effectively.

Practicing transitioning skills through role-playing exercises can significantly enhance adaptability across different contexts. Role-playing allows individuals to simulate real-life communication challenges in a controlled environment, where they can experiment with various styles without fear of real-world consequences.

In these exercises, participants can adopt different personas, such as a demanding client or a skeptical peer, and practice transitioning between communication styles to handle each situation effectively. Such activities can be conducted individually or in group settings, providing valuable feedback and insights into personal strengths and areas for improvement. By consistently engaging in role-playing, communicators cultivate a deeper intuition for style adjustment, readying them for spontaneous challenges in authentic settings.

To refine this adaptability further, it is essential to assess the outcomes of these transitions by analyzing conversational dynamics and soliciting feedback. Understanding the impact of style shifts can provide meaningful insights into what works and what doesn't in different situations.

For example, after a presentation, gathering feedback from colleagues on which parts resonated and which felt out of sync can guide future adjustments. Listening carefully to constructive criticism and recognizing patterns in listener reactions helps fine-tune one's approach. Moreover, reflecting on successful interactions where style transitions were seamless can reinforce positive strategies and encourage ongoing development.

Creating an iterative learning process intertwines closely with assessing transition outcomes. After receiving feedback, practicing refined techniques in subsequent interactions solidifies growth. Imagine attending a networking event where you previously struggled to connect due to overly formal language.

Receiving feedback highlighting your improvement in casual dialogue can bolster confidence for future engagements. This cycle of feedback and practice nurtures continuous enhancement of communication skills, enabling a more natural shift between styles over time.

Incorporating guidelines into these practices provides a structured path for deliberate style transitioning. Techniques such as pausing and pacing transitions benefit greatly from clear guidelines, helping communicators remain focused on their intended goals. It is crucial, however, to avoid overwhelming oneself with excessive rules. Instead, adopting simple, actionable steps for style adaptation ensures greater flexibility and responsiveness during dynamic interactions.

As communicators hone their adaptability, recognizing emotional cues and body language becomes just as important as verbal techniques.

Non-verbal signals often reveal underlying sentiments, guiding the speaker to modify their style even mid-conversation.

For instance, if a listener appears disengaged despite verbal acknowledgment, adjusting the tone or energy level could re-engage them. Similarly, observing attentive body language could signal readiness for more detail or complexity in the discussion.

Key Strategies for Successful Communication Style Adaptation

In an increasingly interconnected world, the ability to adapt communication styles for success involves tailoring messaging to resonate with diverse audiences and environments. A key strategy in achieving this adaptation is cultivating flexibility and openness to differing perspectives. In any professional setting, individuals come from varying backgrounds, each bringing unique ideas and insights. Embracing these differences not only enriches communication but also enhances problem-solving abilities and creativity.

To effectively communicate with diverse groups, it is important to implement adaptable approaches that foster teamwork and collaboration.

For instance, understanding team dynamics and adjusting leadership styles can significantly impact productivity. A flexible leader who empowers team members while respecting their individuality can create an inclusive atmosphere where everyone feels valued and motivated to contribute. This adaptability extends to choosing the right communication channels, whether through face-to-face interactions or digital platforms, depending on what suits the team best at any given moment.

Fostering inclusivity by respecting cultural nuances is another crucial aspect of adapting communication styles. In today's globalized business environment, cultural awareness is essential. Being mindful of cultural norms and traditions helps avoid misunderstandings and fosters trust within the team.

For example, some cultures value direct communication, while others prefer indirect approaches. Recognizing these differences allows professionals to adjust their messaging to be more effective and considerate, ultimately improving relationships and outcomes.

Establishing trust through empathy and active engagement is fundamental for successful communication in diverse interactions. Demonstrating empathy involves placing oneself in another's shoes to understand their experiences and viewpoints. This empathetic approach not only builds rapport but also strengthens bonds between colleagues, clients, and partners.

Active listening is another vital component, as it ensures that all parties feel heard and respected. By actively engaging with diverse perspectives, communication becomes more meaningful and productive.

A practical guideline to promote adaptability is creating opportunities for feedback loops within teams. Regularly seeking feedback provides valuable insights into how communication styles are perceived and where improvements can be made. By analyzing this feedback, individuals can refine their methods to better suit their audience's expectations, thereby enhancing the overall effectiveness of their communication.

Moreover, promoting open dialogues about diversity and inclusion within the workplace encourages a culture where different perspectives are not just tolerated but celebrated. Training sessions focused on cross-cultural communication can equip employees with the skills needed to navigate complex situations and interact respectfully with colleagues from various backgrounds.

Encouraging participation in such initiatives underscores the organization's commitment to fostering an inclusive and adaptive communication environment.

Another strategy involves leveraging technology to bridge communication gaps. Utilizing tools like video conferencing, instant messaging, and collaborative platforms can facilitate real-time communication and reduce potential barriers posed by physical distance or time zones. These tools also offer the flexibility needed to accommodate different working styles and preferences, further supporting teams in achieving their goals.

Building on these strategies, it is vital to recognize the role of emotional intelligence in adapting communication styles. High emotional intelligence enables individuals to read social cues accurately, manage emotions appropriately, and respond to others with sensitivity. This competence fosters an environment where open and honest communication thrives, further reinforcing trust and cooperation among team members.

To ensure enduring success, organizations must support continuous learning and development focused on adaptability in communication. This involves providing resources and training that empower employees to embrace change and remain responsive to emerging trends and challenges. Cultivating a growth mindset encourages individuals to view each interaction as a learning opportunity, motivating them to constantly refine their communication techniques.

Finally, establishing mentorship programs can be instrumental in guiding employees through their journey of developing adaptable communication styles. Mentors can offer personalized advice and share experiences, helping mentees navigate complex interpersonal scenarios with confidence. Such programs foster a sense of community and strengthen the organization's commitment to nurturing diverse talent.

Bringing It All Together

As we conclude this chapter, it's essential to recognize the importance of understanding and adapting communication styles to connect with diverse audiences effectively. Throughout our exploration, we've delved into the significance of personal communication styles—assertive, passive, and aggressive—and how self-awareness can lead to better interactions.

By reflecting on cultural influences and past experiences, individuals gain valuable insights into their communication tendencies, paving the way for improved interpersonal skills and stronger relationships. Recognizing the strengths and weaknesses associated with different styles also allows for strategic enhancements in various settings.

Transitioning into real-world applications, the chapter highlighted the necessity of flexibility when communicating across diverse environments. Understanding the nuances of each situation enables professionals to tailor their messages, whether in a formal meeting or an informal setting. The use of techniques like active listening and mirroring fosters rapport and empathy, ensuring effective and meaningful exchanges.

Additionally, cultural awareness and feedback loops have been emphasized as vital tools for evaluating and refining communication approaches. By integrating these strategies, professionals can enhance teamwork, client interactions, and personal growth, ultimately achieving greater success in both professional and personal spheres.

Chapter 8

Harnessing Emotional Intelligence

Harnessing emotional intelligence is a transformative approach that significantly enriches how individuals interact and communicate with others. By understanding and applying this concept, one can effectively influence relational dynamics and improve interpersonal communications, fostering an environment where clarity and empathy prevail. Emotional intelligence goes beyond mere emotions; it encompasses recognizing, understanding, and managing not only one's own emotions but also those of others. This ability to navigate emotional landscapes can open new avenues for personal growth and professional advancement.

In this chapter, readers will embark on a journey through the core components that make up emotional intelligence, such as self-awareness, self-regulation, motivation, and empathy. The discussion highlights how these elements contribute to cultivating meaningful connections and enhancing communication strategies across various settings.

Through practical examples and relatable scenarios, the chapter illustrates the impact of emotional intelligence on relationship-building and conflict resolution. Readers will gain insights into aligning intrinsic motivations with real-world interactions, thus laying a solid foundation for both personal development and professional success. By exploring these aspects, the chapter aims to equip business professionals, self-improvement enthusiasts, and sales and marketing experts with tools to leverage emotional intelligence effectively in their daily lives.

Components of Emotional Intelligence

Understanding the essence of emotional intelligence in relationships begins with recognizing its key components, starting with self-awareness. Self-awareness is the foundation that helps individuals identify their emotions and understand how these emotions affect not only themselves but also their interactions with others. Becoming self-aware requires a deliberate exploration of one's feelings, thoughts, and behaviors. By identifying and labeling emotions accurately, individuals can communicate more genuinely and effectively, enhancing the quality of their relationships.

For instance, when a person becomes aware of feeling stressed before an important meeting, they might choose to convey their need for patience and understanding from their colleagues, rather than reactively spreading anxiety throughout the team. This level of awareness allows them to maintain authenticity in their communication, fostering trust and transparency within professional or personal settings.

Self-regulation builds on this awareness by enabling individuals to manage their emotional responses constructively. It's about finding the balance between expressing emotions and maintaining effective communication. Those adept at self-regulation do not suppress their feelings; instead, they channel them appropriately depending on the context. This skill is crucial for adapting to changing circumstances and mitigating conflicts. Consider a scenario where two teammates disagree on a project approach. A self-regulated individual might acknowledge their frustration yet refrain from responding impulsively.

Instead, they might express their concerns calmly and propose a trial period for both methods. This constructive interaction can lead to better collaboration and problem-solving, as well as an environment that values diverse viewpoints.

Motivation, another essential component of emotional intelligence, influences how individuals engage in communication and pursue their goals. Intrinsic motivation, which stems from internal desires such as growth and achievement, drives people toward productive dialogues. Unlike extrinsically motivated individuals who might focus solely on immediate rewards like recognition or monetary gain, intrinsically motivated communicators are more likely to persevere through challenges and setbacks.

In a business setting, for example, a salesperson motivated by genuine interest in helping clients will be more inclined to listen attentively and tailor solutions to meet clients' needs. This inner drive fuels meaningful interactions, enhances client satisfaction, and fosters long-term loyalty.

Empathy plays a transformative role by enabling individuals to connect deeply with others' emotions. Understanding and sharing feelings create relatability, making it easier to navigate complex interpersonal dynamics. Empathy involves not only recognizing others' emotions but also appreciating the reasons behind these emotions. It allows one to perceive situations from another person's perspective, a skill invaluable in both personal and professional spheres.

Imagine a marketing professional presenting a new campaign idea. With empathy, they can anticipate potential client concerns and address them proactively during the presentation. This ability to resonate with the audience's feelings results in more engaging presentations and stronger client relationships.

Each of these components—self-awareness, self-regulation, motivation, and empathy—contribute uniquely to relationship-building and communication enhancement. Together, they offer a nuanced understanding of emotional intelligence's pivotal role in creating harmonious and effective relational dynamics.

While mastering these skills may seem daunting, individuals can cultivate them gradually. By regularly reflecting on personal emotions and the impact they have on others, practicing thoughtful responses to emotional stimuli, aligning actions with intrinsic motivations, and seeking to understand varying perspectives, individuals can enhance their emotional intelligence significantly over time.

Benefits of Self-Awareness in Communication

Self-awareness forms the bedrock of emotional intelligence, providing a gateway to enhanced communication. When individuals cultivate a deep understanding of their own emotions, motives, and reactions, they unlock the potential to express themselves with striking clarity. This clarity is not just about choosing the right words but encompasses a full awareness of one's thoughts and feelings. By recognizing these internal states, a person can convey their needs and desires more confidently and effectively, minimizing misunderstandings in both personal and professional interactions.

Consider a scenario where an employee feels overwhelmed by the workload. Without self-awareness, they might express frustration ambiguously, leading to potential conflicts or assumptions by colleagues.

However, a self-aware individual can articulate their challenges clearly, express what support they need, and negotiate solutions that align with their capacity. Such open and precise communication not only resolves immediate issues but also fosters a cooperative workplace environment.

Moreover, self-awareness promotes empowered responses in conversations. It equips individuals to pause and evaluate their reactions before responding, particularly during challenging situations. When an emotionally charged discussion arises, a self-aware person can identify their triggers and choose how best to address them thoughtfully rather than reactively.

This practice minimizes negative exchanges and cultivates a culture of respect and patience. Imagine a team meeting where tensions run high over differing opinions on a project strategy. A team member who lacks self-awareness may react defensively, escalating the conflict.

Conversely, a self-aware participant can assess their initial emotional response, such as irritation, and decide to listen actively instead, seeking to understand others' perspectives before offering a considered opinion. Such deliberate engagement leads to more productive dialogues and strengthens team cohesion.

Increased authenticity, another byproduct of self-awareness, significantly enhances interpersonal connections. Authenticity involves being true to oneself and transparent in interactions, which naturally builds trust and rapport. When individuals are aware of their values and beliefs, they communicate from a place of honesty and integrity. This transparency invites reciprocation, creating a space for genuine relationships to flourish.

For instance, sales professionals who are self-aware can tailor their approaches to resonate with each client's unique needs and preferences. They can reveal their personal stories or insights that genuinely reflect their commitment to the client's success. This authenticity not only inspires trust but also encourages clients to engage openly, laying the groundwork for enduring partnerships.

Furthermore, improved conflict management is a crucial outcome of self-awareness. In any relational dynamic, disagreements are inevitable, but how they are managed determines the strength of the relationship.

Self-aware individuals are equipped to navigate these conflicts with empathy and understanding. They can recognize their emotional states and acknowledge those of others, facilitating discussions that focus on resolution rather than confrontation.

Take the example of two coworkers disputing over resource allocation. A self-aware individual would approach the situation by first identifying their own priorities and biases. They would then engage in active listening, appreciating the other party's viewpoint, and striving to find common ground. This empathetic approach often leads to mutually beneficial solutions and reinforces a culture of collaboration within the organization.

To integrate self-awareness into effective communication, individuals can adopt several practices. Reflection and introspection are fundamental starting points, as they allow individuals to explore their inner landscapes regularly. These practices encourage individuals to assess how their emotions influence their interactions and make adjustments where necessary.

Feedback from peers and mentors provides invaluable insights into how one's communication style impacts others. Constructive feedback helps highlight blind spots and areas for improvement, encouraging continuous growth and adaptation. Additionally, mindfulness techniques, such as meditation and deep breathing, enhance an individual's ability to remain present and composed during interactions, ensuring responses are thoughtful and reasoned.

Managing Emotions in Interactions

Managing emotions during communication is a critical skill for anyone looking to improve their interpersonal interactions. Emotional intelligence plays a pivotal role in ensuring effective communication by allowing us to control and appropriately express our feelings. In particular, recognizing emotional triggers is essential for handling real-time emotional responses.

By being aware of what sets off certain emotions, individuals can prepare themselves mentally to respond calmly rather than react impulsively. This awareness acts as a guiding beacon, helping communicators navigate potentially turbulent situations with more ease.

For instance, if you know that criticism about your work tends to provoke anger, identifying this trigger allows you to preemptively manage the ensuing emotions.

You could remind yourself that the feedback is not personal but rather an opportunity for growth. Such recognition helps in maintaining composure and promotes a productive dialogue. It's like having a roadmap through emotional minefields, thus preventing potential communication breakdowns.

Practicing emotional regulation is another effective strategy. Techniques such as deep breathing, meditation, or even visualizing calming images can significantly contribute to emotional stability.

These practices are not just theoretical; they have physiological benefits. According to research, deep breathing can help lower heart rate and relax the nervous system (Gallo, 2017).

When faced with a stressful conversation, pausing to take a few slow breaths can prevent the sympathetic nervous system from escalating into a 'fight or flight' response. This act of regulation provides a momentary reprieve from the pressure, allowing one to engage more thoughtfully and constructively.

Furthermore, engaging in regular practice of these techniques' conditions the mind and body to respond more adaptively to stressors. For example, regular meditation practitioners often find it easier to remain calm under pressure because they have trained their bodies to enter a relaxed state swiftly. Therefore, incorporating such practices into daily routines not only aids in managing immediate emotional responses but also builds resilience over time.

Seeking feedback from peers is invaluable in improving emotional expression. Constructive criticism from colleagues or friends offers insight into how others perceive your emotional responses. This external perspective can highlight blind spots, allowing for self-improvement. For example, a colleague might point out that during meetings, you tend to dismiss dissenting opinions too quickly, which might be perceived as defensiveness.

In receiving this feedback, you gain a better understanding of how your emotions manifest externally and can adjust accordingly. Open dialogue about emotional responses can foster a culture of trust and collaboration, as it encourages mutual understanding and empathy. Moreover, feedback can serve as a mirror reflecting back aspects of our behavior we might not fully perceive, enabling a more comprehensive approach to emotional management.

Setting intentions before engaging in communication is another potent strategy for emotional management. By clearly defining emotional goals, individuals can direct conversations toward collaborative outcomes. Before entering a discussion, consider what you wish to achieve emotionally. Are you seeking to resolve a conflict? Do you aim to build rapport or communicate something important without confrontation?

Clarifying these goals helps maintain focus and ensures that emotions align with the intended outcomes. For example, if the intention is to resolve a disagreement amicably, approaching the conversation with patience and openness becomes crucial. This intentionality acts as a compass, guiding communications toward positive resolutions. Setting intentions also creates room for reflection post-conversation, allowing one to assess whether the emotional objectives were met and to adjust future approaches accordingly.

Collectively, these strategies form a robust framework for managing emotions during communication, benefiting both personal and professional relationships. By recognizing triggers, practicing emotional regulation, seeking feedback, and setting intentions, individuals equip themselves with tools to handle emotions adeptly. These methods promote not only effective communication but also enhance overall relational dynamics, paving the way for more meaningful interactions.

Using Emotional Intelligence for Conflict Resolution

In the modern world, understanding and managing emotions have become essential skills, particularly in resolving conflicts effectively. Emotional intelligence plays a pivotal role in addressing these challenges by fostering environments conducive to productive conflict resolution. At the heart of emotional intelligence is the capacity to identify underlying emotions in oneself and others. Often conflicts are fueled by unexpressed emotions rather than the issues at hand. By recognizing these emotions, individuals shift their focus from assigning blame to understanding true needs.

For instance, in workplace disagreements, a manager might perceive an employee's resistance as laziness when, in reality, it stems from anxiety or fear of failure. Identifying such emotions not only clarifies the roots of the conflict but also opens pathways for meaningful dialogue. Once emotions are appropriately identified, parties can address deeper concerns, facilitating solutions that satisfy all involved.

Emotional intelligence emphasizes open dialogue as a cornerstone of conflict resolution. Encouraging individuals to express emotions freely fosters an atmosphere where collaborative problem-solving thrives.

When team members feel safe voicing their feelings without fear of judgment, they are more likely to engage in honest communication, paving the way for innovative solutions.

Consider a sales team facing dwindling client engagement; if open discussions reveal that stress levels are causing decreased motivation, managers can implement strategies to alleviate pressure and reinvigorate the team. Through fostering an environment of trust and openness, communication lines remain robust, preventing misunderstandings and enhancing collective outcomes.

The ability to build collaborative solutions further exemplifies the power of emotional intelligence in conflict resolution. Emotionally intelligent individuals prioritize win-win outcomes by focusing on shared goals rather than individual victories. This approach shifts the dynamic from adversarial stances to cooperative engagements.

During negotiations, for example, a marketing professional with high emotional intelligence might frame discussions around mutual benefits, encouraging all parties to explore common interests. Such approaches not only resolve current disputes but also strengthen relationships, ensuring future collaborations are constructive and beneficial.

Moreover, emotionally intelligent individuals view conflict as an avenue for growth rather than merely an obstacle. Every conflict resolution process provides valuable insights for future interactions. Learning from past experiences enhances conflict management skills, equipping individuals with strategies to handle similar situations more adeptly. Reflecting on a disagreement with a client, for instance, may reveal patterns that, once understood, allow for better preparation and adaptation in subsequent encounters. This cycle of learning ensures continuous improvement and adaptability in various conflict scenarios.

Guidelines play an integral role in harnessing emotional intelligence effectively. First, identifying underlying emotions requires patience and active listening. It means setting aside assumptions and approaching conversations with empathy and curiosity. To foster open dialogue, establishing clear communication channels and creating a non-judgmental space is crucial.

Team leaders can initiate this by modeling vulnerability and sharing their experiences, thus encouraging others to follow suit. Building collaborative solutions involves focusing on integrative agreements where all parties' interests are considered. Techniques like brainstorming sessions and joint decision-making processes can facilitate this.

Finally, embracing a mindset of continuous learning helps individuals view conflicts as opportunities for growth. Regular reflection on past interactions and seeking feedback fosters a culture of improvement and innovation.

For business professionals, self-improvement enthusiasts, and those in sales and marketing, developing strong emotional intelligence skills can transform how conflicts are approached and resolved. In the business world, improved relational dynamics lead to better networking, more effective client interactions, and enhanced team dynamics. By leveraging emotional intelligence, professionals can elevate their career trajectories by achieving greater results in their roles.

For self-improvement enthusiasts, mastering emotional intelligence contributes to healthier relationships both professionally and personally. Understanding and managing emotions create a foundation for personal growth and development.

Lastly, for sales and marketing professionals, refining communication techniques through emotional intelligence increases client engagement and retention. Persuasive messaging becomes more authentic and impactful when underpinned by an understanding of emotional cues.

Practical Applications of Emotional Intelligence

Applying emotional intelligence principles in real-world settings can significantly enhance both personal and professional interactions. This chapter delves into how self-awareness, empathy, motivation, and emotional regulation can be harnessed to improve leadership, customer service, mentorship, and public speaking.

Self-awareness is a cornerstone of effective leadership. When leaders understand their emotional triggers, strengths, weaknesses, and the impact they have on others, they are better equipped to guide their teams. Recognizing these elements allows leaders to manage stress and make decisions that align with both personal and organizational values, fostering a positive work culture. For example, a manager aware of their short temper during high-pressure meetings might implement strategies to remain calm, thus preventing a trickle-down effect of stress on their team. By acting as role models, self-aware leaders can encourage open communication and mutual respect, ultimately strengthening team dynamics.

Empathy plays a vital role in customer service by enhancing client satisfaction and loyalty. By resonating with clients' emotions and perspectives, service professionals can tailor their responses to better meet customer needs. In practice, this could mean recognizing when a disgruntled customer is not just upset about a product but also having a bad day.

Addressing their concern with genuine compassion rather than scripted replies can transform a negative experience into a positive one, creating loyal customers more likely to return. Companies like Zappos have built reputations for exceptional customer service through empathy, proving that understanding clients' emotional states can distinguish a brand from its competitors (Sudarshan Somanathan, 2024).

Motivation techniques within mentorship inspire growth and innovation. Mentors who employ emotional intelligence can foster an internal drive among mentees, encouraging a commitment to continuous learning and development. Emotional intelligence helps mentors deliver feedback that is encouraging rather than discouraging. By inspiring others through shared vision and goals, mentors can cultivate environments where creativity thrives.

For instance, a mentor who understands their mentee's passion for sustainability might support this interest by connecting them with projects aligned with their values, sparking enthusiasm and innovative thinking.

Public speaking benefits greatly from emotional regulation, which aids in delivering impactful messages. Speakers who can manage their emotions effectively are better able to convey confidence and engage their audience. Audience members tend to respond positively to speakers who appear calm and composed, even when discussing challenging topics.

Techniques such as deep breathing and visualization can assist speakers in maintaining focus and clarity under pressure. For instance, politicians and motivational speakers often exhibit exceptional emotional control, allowing them to connect deeply with their audiences and leave lasting impressions (Pause Factory & Pause Factory, 2023).

Bringing It All Together

This chapter has delved into the essential components of emotional intelligence and their pivotal role in improving relational dynamics and communication. Emphasizing self-awareness, individuals gain insight into their emotions, facilitating genuine interactions that reduce misunderstandings. Self-regulation takes this a step further by allowing people to manage their emotions effectively, leading to adaptable communication styles that resonate across different professional settings.

Motivation drives individuals toward authentic dialogues powered by intrinsic goals, enhancing perseverance through challenges. Moreover, empathy enables deeper connections by fostering understanding and relatability, which are crucial for navigating complex interpersonal relationships.

By integrating these skills, business professionals can strengthen their networking abilities, enhance client interactions, and foster team cohesion. Self-improvement enthusiasts find avenues for personal growth, building healthier relationships through enhanced emotional intelligence.

For sales and marketing professionals, refining communication techniques through these principles enhances client engagement and retention. Each component of emotional intelligence contributes uniquely, promising not only better individual outcomes but also creating environments where harmonious and effective relationships can thrive. As individuals continue to cultivate these abilities, they can expect to elevate both their personal and professional trajectories significantly.

Chapter 9

Freudian Slips and Speech Patterns: Clues to Underlying Thoughts

Freudian slips and speech patterns unveil the intricate workings of our subconscious mind, offering a window into thoughts and feelings we may not be consciously aware of. These verbal missteps, introduced by Sigmund Freud, serve as more than just amusing anecdotes in conversation; they are significant indicators that reveal the complex layers beneath our spoken words. The chapter will navigate through the fascinating interplay between these slips and speech patterns, showcasing how they can provide clues to hidden intentions and unspoken truths. Through this exploration, readers will encounter a profound understanding of how such communications can influence personal interactions, professional negotiations, and broader societal connections.

The chapter delves into several key dimensions, examining both historical perspectives and practical implications. It begins with an overview of Freudian slips, discussing their roots in psychoanalytic theory and their relevance in modern-day communication analysis. This is followed by an exploration of irregular speech patterns, where habitual language use is linked to emotions and cognitive processes. By presenting real-world examples, the chapter highlights how these elements manifest in various settings, from personal relationships to business environments.

Additionally, the chapter addresses cognitive dissonance, explaining how contradictions between thoughts and words can impact credibility and decision-making. Throughout, there is a focus on cultural interpretations, emphasizing the need for cross-cultural awareness when interpreting these subtle cues.

Ultimately, the chapter offers practical strategies for professionals, self-improvement enthusiasts, and salespeople seeking to enhance communication skills by recognizing and responding to subconscious signals effectively.

Nature of Freudian Slips

The phenomenon of Freudian slips presents a fascinating lens through which one might glimpse the workings of an individual's subconscious. Sigmund Freud introduced this concept, asserting that these verbal blunders are not merely mistakes but windows into hidden desires and unexpressed thoughts. In his landmark work "The Psychopathology of Everyday Life" (Freud, 1901), he suggested that slip-ups occur due to "a disturbing influence of something outside of the intended speech"—namely, unconscious thoughts or repressed emotions.

Understanding the historical context of Freudian slips is crucial for fully appreciating their significance. Freud's theories were groundbreaking, positing that our speech could reveal layers of the mind usually concealed beneath everyday consciousness. He argued that when we blunder in speech, it often results from the temporary lapse in the suppression of these unconscious notions, thereby offering us inadvertent clues about internal conflicts.

The application of Freudian slips extends beyond mere academic interest; they hold considerable significance in various contexts, both personal and professional. In personal settings, such as relationships, slips can inadvertently disclose one's true feelings about a partner, family member, or friend.

For example, slipping by calling a current partner by an ex's name may unveil lingering attachments or unresolved emotions. In professional scenarios, a slip can indicate stress, dissatisfaction, or underlying concerns about work dynamics. This revelation can be quite telling during meetings or negotiations where careful communication is paramount.

Professionals across fields have recognized the potential of Freudian slips as tools for deeper insight and discussion. Therapists and psychologists, in particular, use slips as conversation starters or diagnostic indicators to explore their clients' unvoiced anxieties or desires. They offer an opening into what individuals might otherwise keep hidden, facilitating dialogue around issues that might be difficult to address directly. It becomes evident that what at first seems incidental may carry substantial weight in understanding a person's psyche.

Real-life examples further illustrate how Freudian slips operate in practice. One famous incident involved Senator Ted Kennedy during a televised speech on education; instead of saying "the best and brightest," he mistakenly said "breast." The slip was accompanied by a hand gesture that appeared to mimic cupping, adding another layer to its unintended message. His quick correction didn't erase the split-second peek into the subconscious display of whatever associations his mind made at that moment (Nickerson, 2022).

Another notable example occurred with Pope Francis, who, during a Vatican sermon, accidentally used a vulgar Italian word similar in pronunciation to the intended term "example." Despite quickly correcting himself, the slip gained viral attention, highlighting how even revered figures can experience these involuntary revelations. Similarly, former National Security Advisor Condoleezza Rice once referred to President Bush as her "husb—," before correcting herself, providing a window, intentional or not, into potential subconscious musings.

These instances of Freudian slips remind us of the fragile boundary between the conscious and subconscious minds. While modern research still debates the extent to which slips are directly linked to deeply repressed desires, they are undeniably part of the fabric of human psychological complexity (Cherry, 2019). Observationally, slips might arise from heightened states of distraction, anxiety, or emotional overwhelm, all of which facilitate lapses in verbal control that allow the subconscious to peek through.

For business professionals, self-improvement enthusiasts, and sales or marketing professionals looking to refine their interpersonal communications, understanding Freudian slips provides a framework for interpreting subtle cues in both themselves and others. Recognizing these slips can aid in fostering better rapport with clients, navigating team dynamics more effectively, and tailoring persuasive messaging that resonates authentically with audiences.

Analyzing Irregular Speech Patterns

Understanding speech patterns is a fascinating venture into the depths of human communication, revealing underlying emotions and intentions that may not be immediately apparent. By examining habitual speech, we can begin to link it to personality traits or stress levels, offering insights into how people express their subconscious thoughts.

For example, frequent use of certain phrases or changes in tone might suggest anxiety or confidence levels, while pauses or hesitations can indicate uncertainty or internal conflict. The way individuals communicate is often closely tied to their emotional states. Research has demonstrated that stressed individuals tend to exhibit less linguistic cognitive complexity, suggesting that their ability to articulate thoughts diminishes under pressure (Saslow et al., 2013).

This insight can be particularly valuable for business professionals seeking to fine-tune their interpersonal interactions by recognizing these patterns in themselves and others.

To bring these concepts to life, we can look at case studies where speech irregularities have profoundly impacted business outcomes. In high-stakes environments, misinterpretation of speech cues can lead to significant misunderstandings.

For instance, a manager who speaks rapidly during meetings might unintentionally convey stress or impatience, influencing the team's perception and performance. On the other hand, a salesperson who carefully modulates their tone and pace can project calm and reliability, increasing client trust and engagement.

In one illustrative case, an executive noticed decreased productivity and morale within her team. Through careful observation, she identified that her own expedited communication style was causing confusion and stress among team members. By slowing down her speech and actively listening, she was able to foster a more conducive atmosphere for collaboration, ultimately improving project outcomes and team dynamics.

Analyzing such cases highlights the necessity of developing strategies for addressing speech patterns. One effective technique is mindfulness in communication—practicing active listening and deliberate speech can enhance clarity and reduce misinterpretations. Utilizing breathing exercises before speaking engagements or meetings can help maintain composure and prevent hurried or unclear delivery.

Moreover, encouraging open dialogue around communication styles within teams can promote awareness and adaptability. Coaching sessions focused on public speaking or providing constructive feedback can empower individuals to refine their speech delivery, leading to improved professional relationships and increased self-awareness. These strategies can also benefit sales and marketing professionals striving to enhance client retention through persuasive yet genuine messaging.

Feedback loops play a crucial role in refining communication effectiveness. When individuals receive well-articulated feedback on their communication patterns, they gain valuable insights into areas requiring improvement. This ongoing process encourages continuous development and adaptation, ensuring that communication remains aligned with desired goals.

A practical implementation of feedback loops can be seen in team settings where regular meetings are held specifically to discuss communication successes and challenges. By creating a safe environment for sharing experiences and suggestions, teams can develop a culture of constant growth and improvement.

This collaborative approach not only strengthens interpersonal relationships but also enhances overall organizational efficiency. Ultimately, the ability to analyze variations in speech provides a powerful tool for unlocking deeper understanding and fostering effective communication. Whether in personal or professional contexts, recognizing the subtle nuances of speech empowers individuals to navigate complex interactions with greater empathy and insight. As our awareness of these patterns grows, so too does our capacity to connect meaningfully with those around us, paving the way for richer, more fulfilling relationships.

Indicators of Cognitive Dissonance

Cognitive dissonance, a concept rooted in social psychology, provides profound insights into the inconsistencies between thoughts and words. Initially conceptualized by Leon Festinger, this theory describes the discomfort people feel when they simultaneously hold contradictory beliefs or attitudes. Such internal conflicts often manifest during communication, affecting trust and altering interpersonal dynamics.

When individuals express ideas that clash with their core values or beliefs, listeners might sense an inconsistency that triggers doubt about the speaker's authenticity. For business professionals, who rely on clear and trustworthy communication, understanding these manifestations is crucial.

The signs of cognitive dissonance become apparent in both verbal and non-verbal cues. Verbally, individuals may exhibit hesitation, frequent self-correction, or over-justification in their speech.

For instance, someone might say, "I usually agree, but..." which indicates an underlying conflict. Non-verbally, signs such as avoiding eye contact, nervous gestures, or an altered tone of voice can reveal dissonance.

Recognizing these indicators allows practitioners to better understand the complex layers of communication occurring in real-time. Cognitive dissonance has notable implications for decision-making, particularly in high-pressure environments like negotiations. During negotiations, parties involved must align their spoken words with their actual intentions and beliefs.

However, when dissonance exists, it can complicate decision-making processes. For example, a negotiator might internally believe that conceding on certain points would harm their position, yet outwardly they might feel pressured to appear cooperative. This internal struggle can lead to decisions that are not fully supported by their core beliefs, potentially undermining their negotiation stance and leading to regretful outcomes.

Recognizing these patterns can be particularly advantageous in sales and marketing. Professionals in these fields often encounter clients who exhibit signs of dissonance when faced with purchasing decisions. A client hesitating between two products might verbally justify one choice while their non-verbal cues indicate preference for another.

An astute salesperson, detecting this subtle discord, can pivot their strategy to address these conflicting signals, thereby fostering a more sincere client interaction that aligns with the client's true preferences.

Applications in conflict resolution further underscore the importance of understanding cognitive dissonance. Conflicts, whether personal or professional, frequently arise from unacknowledged dissonance between expressed views and true feelings.

By employing tools that identify these discrepancies, mediators can facilitate discussions that reveal deeper truths and foster mutual understanding.

Active listening techniques that focus on comprehensive observation of both verbal and non-verbal cues are invaluable here. They can uncover underlying tensions, enabling conflicting parties to articulate their genuine concerns and motivations.

In practice, leveraging insights into cognitive dissonance can transform how conflicts are approached. Imagine a workplace scenario where two team members consistently disagree on project directions. While one member vocalizes support for innovative approaches, their body language suggests apprehension.

Identifying this inconsistency opens avenues for dialogue focused on exploring hidden reservations and finding common ground. By addressing the root cause of dissonance, teams can progress towards resolutions that genuinely resonate with all stakeholders.

Furthermore, guidelines for recognizing dissonance are essential for enhancing interpersonal communications. Business professionals, self-improvement enthusiasts, and sales personnel alike can benefit from cultivating awareness of the signs and implications of cognitive dissonance.

Developing skills in active listening, empathy, and observational acumen enhances one's ability to detect and respond to dissonance effectively. Encouraging environments where open expression of thoughts and feelings is welcomed can reduce the need for defensive communication, thus minimizing cognitive dissonance.

Cultural Perspectives on Freudian Slips

Freudian slips, often seen as inadvertent errors in speech, can serve as windows into the subconscious mind. However, their interpretation varies significantly across different cultures, highlighting the need to understand cultural nuances to avoid misinterpretations. When viewed through the lens of cultural diversity, the impact and meaning of Freudian slips can change dramatically.

Various cultural backgrounds interpret these slips differently, either as simple errors or as significant reflections of hidden thoughts. In some Eastern cultures, for example, there might be less emphasis on Freudian psychology, leading to interpretations of slips as mere mistakes rather than subconscious revelations.

Meanwhile, Western societies, particularly those influenced by psychoanalytic theories, might view such errors as significant insights into one's internal conflicts.

The way in which people respond to Freudian slips also depends heavily on the social context in which they occur. Social settings, whether formal or informal, play a crucial role in determining reactions to these slips. In a professional environment, a slip of the tongue might lead to embarrassment or even suspicion about underlying intentions (Supertext, n.d.).

Conversely, in casual conversations among friends, such slips may result in laughter and be easily dismissed as unintended mistakes. This variance underscores the importance of considering the context in which a slip occurs when trying to understand its implications.

Given these variations, culturally sensitive strategies are essential when addressing Freudian slips. One approach could involve acknowledging the slip without dwelling on it, thereby respecting cultural norms that lean towards discretion and informality.

For instance, in situations where a slip could potentially cause offense, such as in diplomatic dialogues, careful phrasing and acknowledgment can help maintain harmony and prevent misunderstandings. Acknowledging the difference between intent and spoken word can diffuse tension and promote understanding.

Freudian slips can also have significant implications for global communication. As our world becomes increasingly interconnected, the ability to recognize and appropriately respond to these slips is vital for enhancing international interactions.

In business meetings involving multicultural teams, understanding that a Freudian slip might not necessarily convey true intent can foster a more forgiving and open communication environment. This awareness allows individuals to navigate complex communications with greater ease and tolerance.

For instance, sales and marketing professionals who frequently engage with clients from diverse backgrounds can benefit from this understanding, ensuring that unintended slips do not jeopardize relationships or negotiations.

Furthermore, recognizing the importance of cultural interpretations of Freudian slips enhances emotional intelligence. Self-improvement enthusiasts committed to personal growth can strengthen interpersonal skills by embracing cultural awareness.

By being mindful of varying interpretations, they can cultivate empathy and adaptability in both professional and personal spheres, fostering stronger connections and reducing potential conflicts.

Practical Applications in Business Settings

Navigating the subtle cues embedded within speech patterns can be a game-changer in professional environments. Freudian slips, often unintended errors that reveal subconscious thoughts, along with speech analysis, can unveil hidden intentions and emotions. For those aiming to enhance their interpersonal prowess, understanding these nuances offers a valuable edge. Incorporating techniques like active listening and tactical empathy in meetings allows professionals to guide conversations more effectively. This approach emphasizes not only what's being said but also how it's conveyed.

Professionals can elevate meetings by delving into speech analysis to extract underlying messages. Start with active listening—engaging deeply with what's spoken to grasp the essence of the message. By honing in on tone shifts, hesitations, or repeated phrases, leaders can better steer discussions, ensuring they align with organizational goals.

One effective method is mirroring, which involves repeating key points back to the speaker, validating their input while subtly directing the conversation's flow. Such techniques foster an environment where ideas flourish, driving meeting efficacy.

The realm of negotiation benefits significantly from awareness of cognitive dissonance, where what someone says may not align with their true beliefs. Recognizing this dissonance is crucial for negotiating effectively. Often, negotiators focus too much on their arguments, missing signals of internal conflict in their counterparts.

Instead, wise negotiators prioritize the other party's discourse, attuning themselves to inconsistencies that might indicate areas ripe for compromise. Patience is key; slowing down negotiations can help identify genuine needs, leading to mutually beneficial outcomes.

Building robust client relationships requires interpreting subconscious signals accurately. In sales, subtle speech patterns can betray a client's hesitance or enthusiasm, providing invaluable insights beyond textual exchanges.

For instance, clients might express excitement verbally yet sound lukewarm, hinting at reservations. Sales professionals should cultivate emotional intelligence to discern these clues, adapting their strategies accordingly. This might involve empathetic questioning, inviting clients to share concerns candidly, thus nurturing trust and long-term engagement.

Furthermore, creating a team culture that values communication refinement can significantly impact performance. Implementing feedback strategies centered around speech pattern analysis fosters a culture of continuous improvement. Regular feedback sessions focusing on verbal communication can illuminate areas for development, enhancing team collaboration.

A practical guideline would involve establishing norms where constructive critiques are welcomed. Encouraging team members to reflect on their communication styles and offering peer feedback can lead to more cohesive and effective teamwork. Emphasizing empathy and open dialogue also promotes a supportive environment where individuals feel heard and valued.

When teams practice giving and receiving feedback well, they cultivate resilience and innovation. Ensuring feedback is specific and actionable, rather than general and vague, helps drive meaningful change. As teams become adept at recognizing how speech impacts dynamics, they build a stronger collective identity, ultimately improving organizational success.

Bringing It All Together

As we draw this chapter to a close, we've delved deeply into the intriguing concept of subconscious signals in speech, shedding light on how these can reveal underlying intentions and emotions. By examining elements such as Freudian slips, irregular speech patterns, and cognitive dissonance, we've uncovered how these inadvertent cues offer a wealth of information about interpersonal dynamics.

For business professionals, self-improvement enthusiasts, and sales or marketing specialists, understanding these aspects is pivotal for refining communication strategies. These insights provide concrete tools for navigating conversations more effectively, whether in negotiating successful outcomes, improving team dynamics, or building lasting client relationships.

Moreover, our exploration emphasized the importance of cultural perspectives and practical applications in business settings. We've seen that recognizing subconscious signals across different cultural contexts can enrich communication and prevent misunderstandings.

Furthermore, the practical applications discussed highlight techniques like active listening, mirroring, and empathy, which are instrumental in unlocking deeper connections. As readers integrate these concepts into their professional and personal lives, they will enhance their ability to interact meaningfully and empathetically, paving the way for more fulfilling and productive relationships.

Chapter 10

Applying Communication Skills in Business Contexts

Applying communication skills in business contexts is essential for achieving success in sales, client retention, and professional relationships. Effective communication serves as the foundation upon which meaningful interactions are built, facilitating a deeper understanding between businesses and their clients or partners. In this chapter, readers will delve into various strategies that enhance communication effectiveness within business settings, offering practical insights to refine interpersonal skills crucial for both career advancement and personal growth.

The focus is not merely on transmitting information but on engaging with others in ways that resonate and foster long-lasting connections. For professionals aiming to excel in their fields, mastering these skills can lead to more productive networking, improved teamwork, and successful client engagements, ultimately contributing to greater career satisfaction and success.

The chapter explores several key aspects of business communication, starting with techniques designed to elevate sales communications by tailoring messages to match client needs and motivations. It emphasizes the importance of active listening and effective questioning to uncover client desires that may not be immediately apparent. Readers will learn how building trust through authenticity and relatability can transform sales pitches into compelling narratives that speak to the heart of the client's challenges and aspirations. Furthermore, the chapter provides guidance on crafting proposals that prioritize benefits over features, ensuring that messaging aligns with the client's goals and values.

As the discussion progresses, the chapter introduces methods for closing deals through empowering questioning techniques that involve clients in decision-making processes without applying pressure. These strategies collectively equip business professionals with the tools needed to drive sales, retain clients, and forge strong professional relationships, enhancing their overall communication prowess in business contexts.

Effective Sales Communication Techniques

Crafting messages that not only engage clients but also drive sales requires a deep understanding of various communication strategies aimed at resonating with the client's desires and motivations. At the core of effective sales communication is recognizing what the client truly needs, which often goes beyond their immediate spoken requirements. Understanding these underlying desires is crucial as it enables tailored messaging that speaks directly to the client's heart, making them feel heard and valued.

One fundamental way to uncover these needs is through active listening and effective questioning techniques. Engaging clients in conversations where you gently probe deeper into their motivations can illuminate their true needs. This approach moves beyond surface-level engagement and allows for crafting messages that resonate on a personal level, ultimately leading to more meaningful interactions and successful outcomes.

Building trust and rapport is another cornerstone of effective communication in business contexts. Trust is the foundation upon which all successful transactions are built. One practical method of building this trust is through sharing personal anecdotes. These stories foster a sense of relatability and authenticity.

When clients see you as a person rather than just a salesperson, they are more likely to open up about their own experiences and needs. This exchange creates a comfortable environment where authentic connections flourish, increasing client comfort levels and fostering long-term relationships.

Once client needs are understood and trust is established, the next step involves crafting compelling proposals. A common pitfall in sales messaging is focusing too heavily on the features of a product or service. While features are important, what's more impactful is highlighting the benefits those features provide.

Clients want to know how your offering will solve their problems or enhance their lives. By shifting the focus from what your product is to what your product does for the client, you ensure that the message resonates with their values and priorities. For example, instead of saying, "This software has advanced data analytics capabilities," reframe it to emphasize the benefit: "This software helps you gain crucial insights into customer behavior, allowing for more targeted marketing strategies." This shift from feature-centric to benefit-focused messaging makes the proposal more engaging, as clients can easily recognize the value being offered.

As the conversation progresses towards closing the deal, it's vital to employ questioning strategies that empower the clients rather than pressure them. Effective closing techniques involve asking open-ended questions that encourage clients to verbalize their thoughts and feelings about the proposal.

Questions like, "What do you think would be the most beneficial part of this solution for your team?" or "How do you see this fitting into your current strategy?" invite the client to take an active role in the decision-making process.

Empowering clients in this way not only reduces the pressure associated with making a purchase but also ensures they feel in control, which can significantly increase the likelihood of closing the sale. Furthermore, by asking such questions, you're able to gather valuable feedback that could be used to refine your offering or approach in future interactions.

In summary, the journey to creating effective sales messages begins with understanding the client's true needs, building trust through relatability, crafting proposals that highlight benefits over features, and utilizing empowering questioning techniques during the closing phase. By focusing on these key areas, business professionals can craft messages that not only engage clients but also drive sales effectively, enhancing both client relationships and professional success.

To successfully execute these strategies, it's essential to integrate research into your sales workflow. Gathering comprehensive information about your products, market trends, and competitors equips your sales team with the necessary knowledge to tailor pitches that align with client expectations and industry standards (Shekhar, 2022). Simultaneously, defining clear and concise messaging ensures clarity and effectiveness, avoiding unnecessary information that may dilute the message's impact.

Moreover, leveraging the appropriate communication channels is crucial. Selecting the right medium—be it email, social media, or face-to-face meetings—can amplify the message's reach and effectiveness, ensuring it resonates with the target audience. Equally important is maintaining a follow-up strategy that strikes a balance between persistence and respect for the client's time, keeping your brand at the forefront of their minds without being intrusive.

Best Practices for Client Retention

In a world where business landscapes are ever-evolving, maintaining strong relationships with clients stands paramount for success. Building long-term connections not only fosters client loyalty but also propels businesses to new heights. This discussion focuses on strategies that solidify ongoing relationships, ensuring lasting success.

Regular check-ins are foundational for preventing client disengagement. These interactions don't have to be extensive; they simply need to be consistent. Implementing scheduled follow-ups allows you to stay on your clients' radar, showing them that their needs and satisfaction are priorities.

For instance, a monthly or quarterly check-in can take the form of personalized emails or phone calls. These conversations should aim to reassure clients of their importance and invite them to express any concerns or questions they might have. Keeping this line of communication open fosters trust, making clients feel valued and heard.

Beyond regular check-ins, offering value-added services is crucial. While the primary goal might be sales, providing industry insights through newsletters or hosting informational events can elevate the relationship from transactional to collaborative. Newsletters can include trends, expert opinions, and case studies relevant to the client's industry.

Similarly, organizing webinars or workshops tailored to their interests encourages client engagement by aligning them with your brand's expertise. This approach not only deepens the client-business relationship but positions you as a thought leader who is invested in their ongoing success.

Another pivotal strategy involves actively soliciting feedback post-interaction. Feedback serves as a compass, guiding you to understand areas of satisfaction and those requiring improvement. Utilizing surveys after a project or service completion helps collect valuable insights directly from clients. These surveys should be simple, focusing on key aspects of the interaction, such as the quality of service, communication effectiveness, and overall client experience. Encouraging honest responses ensures a clearer perspective on client emotions and expectations.

Implementing changes based on this feedback demonstrates your commitment to continual improvement, increasing client satisfaction and loyalty over time. It's vital to reassure clients that their opinions are not just heard but translated into meaningful action.

Problem resolution is another critical aspect of nurturing client relationships. Issues or misunderstandings may arise, but how they're handled can make or break the relationship. An effective problem resolution strategy starts with acknowledging the concern promptly. Once identified, addressing the issue with empathy and a collaborative mindset is essential.

Developing solutions together reinforces trust and showcases a willingness to adapt practices for the client's benefit. It's crucial to remain open to suggestions and demonstrate flexibility in modifying processes to resolve the issue amicably. This collaborative problem-solving approach turns potentially negative situations into opportunities for strengthening the partnership.

A unique aspect of fostering long-term relationships lies in building trust and rapport. Trust, once established, paves the way for open communication and mutual respect. Being transparent about the objectives and challenges of projects and managing client expectations realistically contributes to a trusting environment. Ensuring your actions align with your words reassures clients of your reliability and fortifies the bond between you. This trust can be built gradually through consistency in delivering promised results and maintaining professionalism at every touchpoint.

Creating a genuine interest in the client's success is another effective approach. This can be achieved by taking the time to understand both their short-term and long-term goals and exploring how your offerings align with these aspirations.

This understanding enables you to tailor your services strategically, offering them personalized solutions that resonate with their specific needs. Demonstrating enthusiasm for their achievements further strengthens the relationship, showcasing your investment in their progress beyond just the business transaction.

Building Authentic Relationships

In the realm of business, authenticity plays a pivotal role in forming lasting relationships. The ability to be genuine in our communications not only fosters trust but also cultivates respect among professionals. Authenticity is not about wearing a façade; rather, it is about presenting one's true self in interactions, thereby creating an atmosphere where collaboration and understanding can thrive. Being genuine in communication means expressing oneself honestly and transparently. In the fast-paced world of business, honesty builds credibility.

For instance, when a salesperson communicates with a potential client, acknowledging both the strengths and limitations of a product demonstrates integrity.

This openness establishes a foundation of trust because clients are more likely to respect someone who is upfront about potential challenges and committed to finding solutions. Scott Van Voorhis from Harvard Business School emphasizes this by pointing out that fostering a high-trust organization starts with leadership being transparent and authentic (Lewis, 2022).

Respecting individual differences is another cornerstone of building robust business relationships. Every person we encounter comes with their unique perspectives shaped by their culture, experiences, and personal values. Thus, adapting communication styles to accommodate these differences can prevent misunderstandings.

For example, when interacting with colleagues or clients from diverse backgrounds, it is crucial to listen actively and respond in ways that acknowledge and respect their viewpoints. By doing so, you communicate not just with words but with empathy, which enhances mutual understanding and strengthens bonds. Consistency in communication is equally essential. When individuals know they can rely on predictable and transparent interactions, confidence in professional commitments is reinforced. Imagine working with a team leader who consistently follows through on promises and maintains clear communication channels. Such reliability instils a sense of security and stability, vital for long-term business relationships. Being consistent means ensuring your actions align with your words, which is often how professionalism is perceived and valued. Creating collaborative environments by involving clients in decision-making processes further strengthens partnerships. Collaboration does not merely happen; it requires deliberate effort to include others in discussions and respect their contributions.

Consider a marketing campaign where the client's insights are sought and integrated into the strategy. This inclusive approach not only enriches the final product but also makes the client feel valued and heard, fostering a sense of partnership. It transforms transactional relationships into partnerships grounded in mutual respect and shared objectives.

Moreover, fostering such collaborations often leads to innovative solutions. When varying perspectives come together, new ideas emerge, benefitting all parties involved. Effective collaboration relies on open lines of communication where feedback is encouraged and appreciated. As highlighted in source 2, practicing transparency and maintaining open communication channels cultivates creativity and innovation, leading to enhanced team performance. To truly harness the power of authenticity, one must also embrace vulnerability. Leaders who share their experiences, including failures, create an environment where others feel safe to express their ideas without fear of judgment. This kind of authenticity encourages learning and growth within teams. Vulnerability does not equate to weakness; rather, it reflects courage and humility—qualities that enhance relationships and drive engagement.

Implementing these principles effectively can transform workplace dynamics. Business professionals seeking to enhance their interpersonal skills will find that authentic communication aids not only in improving networking capabilities but also in cementing client interactions. For sales and marketing professionals, authenticity becomes a tool for refining communication techniques to boost client engagement and retention. These strategies are particularly potent in today's ever-evolving business landscape, where adaptability and emotional intelligence are highly valued.

For those committed to self-improvement, embracing authenticity offers profound personal growth opportunities. It allows individuals to develop deeper connections within themselves and with others, both professionally and personally. Authenticity challenges us to align our actions with our beliefs and values, leading to a more fulfilling work experience.

Communication Strategies in Marketing

In today's dynamic marketplace, understanding your audience is paramount to crafting effective marketing campaigns. This process begins with thorough market research, providing invaluable insights into the needs, preferences, and behaviors of potential customers. By segmenting audiences based on demographics, psychographics, and purchasing behavior, businesses can develop targeted strategies that speak directly to the individuals they're trying to reach.

Imagine a scenario where a company markets running shoes; by identifying specific segments such as professional athletes versus casual joggers, they can tailor messages that align with each group's unique interests and motivations. Market research not only informs these strategies but also helps in building personalized messaging that resonates with the audience's specific demands.

Storytelling is another powerful tool in a marketer's arsenal, crucial for creating impactful narratives that connect emotionally with clients. Unlike dry pitches or mere presentations of product features, storytelling weaves a narrative fabric rich with characters, conflicts, and resolutions.

Consider how a tech company might share a story about a small business owner who uses their software to overcome daily challenges, achieving growth and success. Such stories humanize brands, making them relatable and engaging. They provide context and meaning, transforming abstract concepts like 'innovation' or 'efficiency' into tangible experiences. Through storytelling, businesses can convey their values, mission, and the benefits of their products in ways that attract attention and foster loyalty.

An integrated multi-channel approach further amplifies communication effectiveness. By consistently delivering messages across various platforms, businesses ensure that their brand voice remains uniform, strengthening recognition and trust (Lindley, 2023). This strategy caters to the modern consumer's behavior, as individuals now interact with brands through multiple touchpoints—social media, emails, websites, and more.

A multi-channel approach allows companies to meet their customers wherever they are, whether scrolling through Instagram, reading newsletters, or browsing online stores. For instance, a brand launching a new product can synchronize its efforts through email campaigns, social media posts, and in-store promotions, ensuring a cohesive message that captures attention across all fronts. The goal is a seamless customer experience, making interactions with the brand both satisfying and memorable.

Encouraging engagement and interaction through feedback opportunities is essential for fostering an active dialogue with consumers. Feedback loops not only make customers feel heard but also provide businesses with critical insights into consumer satisfaction and areas needing improvement. Implementing surveys, comment sections, or interactive content like polls and quizzes encourages customers to share their opinions and preferences.

For example, a restaurant may ask diners to complete a quick survey about their dining experience, offering incentives like discounts on future visits. This not only gathers valuable feedback but also strengthens the relationship between the business and its patrons by demonstrating a commitment to listening and adapting to customer needs.

Incorporating interactive elements in marketing campaigns enhances consumer involvement, turning passive observers into active participants. These interactions go beyond simple advertisements by encouraging users to engage with content and share it within their networks.

Take, for instance, a furniture company that hosts virtual design workshops online, inviting participants to collaborate and showcase their designs using the company's products. Such initiatives not only generate interest but also cultivate a sense of community around the brand, as participants feel part of something larger. Engaging directly with the audience also provides rich data sources that help refine marketing strategies, ensuring they remain aligned with evolving consumer preferences (Public, 2024).

Feedback from these interactions becomes instrumental in optimizing future campaigns. By analyzing responses, marketers can gauge what resonates with different segments and adjust their approaches accordingly. If a clothing label finds that customers love their eco-friendly packaging, they might emphasize this feature more prominently in future marketing materials. This iterative process of testing and tweaking ensures that communication strategies evolve alongside customer expectations and market trends, ultimately maximizing the impact of marketing efforts.

Bringing It All Together

This chapter explored pivotal strategies to enhance communication effectiveness across various professional landscapes, such as sales, client retention, and building authentic relationships. Central to this discourse were techniques like active listening, effective questioning, and the importance of weaving personal anecdotes into sales conversations to foster trust and relatability.

By understanding clients' deeper needs and focusing on benefits rather than features, business professionals can formulate compelling propositions that resonate with their audience's core values. Equally important is empowering clients in decision-making processes, ensuring they feel heard and valued, thus paving the way for meaningful client engagement and successful transactions.

Furthermore, sustainable client relationships are built on regular check-ins, offering value-added services, and embracing transparency. Through these methods, businesses can transform transactional interactions into collaborative partnerships, enhancing trust and loyalty.

Utilizing storytelling in marketing, along with integrated multi-channel approaches, bolsters client connection by creating relatable narratives and consistent brand messaging. Feedback plays a critical role here, providing insights for continuous improvement and fostering a sense of belonging among clients. Ultimately, the strategies outlined emphasize the importance of genuine communication, adaptability, and emotional intelligence in forming lasting professional connections and achieving business success.

Conclusion

As we conclude this journey through the art and science of mastering communication, it's essential to reflect on the key insights we've gathered along the way. Each chapter of this book has been crafted with the intent to guide you through the complexities and nuances that define effective interpersonal communication, whether it is in a business context, personal relationships, or educational pursuits.

First and foremost, we must recognize that communication is not a singular skill but a multifaceted set of abilities that include listening, interpreting non-verbal cues, and fostering genuine empathy. Throughout our exploration, we have delved into how these aspects intertwine and create a robust framework for interactions that can transform both personal and professional realms.

Imagine, for instance, stepping into a networking event with newfound confidence. No longer is it just about exchanging business cards; it's an opportunity to engage in meaningful conversations where active listening becomes your superpower. By paying close attention to what is being said—and what is not—you can navigate these interactions more effectively, building connections that are based on mutual understanding and respect.

This is particularly crucial for business professionals who seek to elevate their careers by enhancing client interactions and team dynamics. Empathy emerges as a critical cornerstone of communication. It goes beyond simply hearing the words spoken; it involves tuning into the emotional undertones that accompany them. Empathy allows us to better understand those around us, whether they be colleagues, clients, friends, or family members. Consider a scenario where a coworker might seem distracted during a meeting.

An empathetic approach would prompt you to inquire gently about their well-being, perhaps uncovering challenges they face that require a compassionate response. Herein lies the power of empathy to forge deeper connections and resolve potential conflicts before they even arise—a powerful tool for self-improvement enthusiasts dedicated to personal growth.

In applying these skills, practice is imperative. Communication is akin to any other discipline—it requires continual effort and refinement. Every conversation presents an opportunity to hone your abilities further. Visualize yourself entering each dialogue with the intention of practicing active listening, responding thoughtfully, and adapting your approach as needed.

Over time, this commitment can lead to transformative results, opening doors to unexpected breakthroughs and fostering stronger relationships across various contexts. For sales and marketing professionals, this translates into enhanced client engagement and retention, thereby solidifying long-term relationships. Professionally, the call to action is clear: integrate the techniques discussed within these pages into your daily routines. Whether you're leading a team meeting, negotiating a contract, or simply making small talk at a networking event, consider how you can incorporate mindful communication practices.

By focusing on how your verbal and non-verbal cues contribute to the atmosphere of each interaction, you can cultivate an environment of trust and collaboration—essentials for anyone juggling multiple responsibilities and seeking to optimize productivity.

Beyond the workplace, the principles outlined in this book extend to personal and familial spheres as well. Parents balancing family duties alongside career ambitions can benefit greatly from improved communication strategies. Whether it's navigating discussions with children or coordinating household responsibilities with partners, empathetic and clear exchanges promote harmony and understanding at home.

For lifelong learners and students, enhanced communication serves as a catalyst for better educational outcomes. When equipped with effective listening and expression skills, the ability to retain and process information improves significantly, leading to greater academic success and intellectual satisfaction.

Ultimately, the pursuit of enhanced communication is a journey without a finite end. It's an ongoing commitment to personal and professional development that pays dividends over time. As you step forward, armed with the knowledge and tools provided in this book, embrace every interaction as a chance to grow and excel as a communicator. Recall the insights you've gained, the techniques you've learned, and apply them diligently.

Consider setting small, achievable goals to track your progress. Reflect regularly on your experiences and adjust your approaches accordingly. Celebrate the successes, no matter how minor they may seem, and learn from the setbacks, using them as stepping stones toward improvement. Your persistence is key to transforming theory into practice.

Moreover, share your journey with others. Engage in discussions with peers or colleagues who might also benefit from this knowledge. Collaboration not only reinforces learning but also builds a supportive community of like-minded individuals striving for excellence in communication.

Remember that communication is ultimately about connection. It is about bridging gaps, resolving misunderstandings, and fostering authentic relationships. Whether you're engaging in a high-stakes business negotiation, comforting a friend, or simply striving to be a better listener, each moment is an opportunity to make a positive impact.

As you conclude this book and prepare for your next conversation, envision the communicator you aspire to become. Approach each interaction with an open mind, a sense of curiosity, a willingness to embrace discomfort, and a sincere desire to connect. By doing so, you will not only enhance your own life but also bring value to the lives of those around you. Let this be your call to action: to integrate effective communication into the fabric of your daily existence, to never cease practicing and improving, and to always strive for deeper understanding and empathy in every exchange. Embrace the challenge, and watch as the world opens up to new possibilities, one conversation at a time.

References

Ashman, M. (2018). Communication models – Introduction to Professional Communications. Bccampus.ca. https://pressbooks.bccampus.ca/professionalcomms/chapter/3-2-the-communication-process-communication-in-the-real-world-an-introduction-to-communication-studies/

Barnhill, A. (2024, August 12). Council Post: Effective Communication: How Leaders Can Inspire, Engage And Succeed. Forbes. https://www.forbes.com/councils/forbescoachescouncil/2023/07/21/effective-communication-how-leaders-can-inspire-engage-and-succeed/

Bernard, K. (2023, March 23). Feedback in Communication: The Complete Workplace Guide. Primalogik. https://primalogik.com/blog/feedback-communication-complete-guide/

Biesenbach, R. (2021, December 1). How to Control Your Emotions When Speaking: 10 Tips. Rob Biesenbach. https://robbiesenbach.com/2021/12/01/how-to-control-your-emotions-when-speaking-10-tips/

Binsaeed, R. H., Yousaf, Z., Grigorescu, A., Condrea, E., & Nassani, A. A. (2023, July 1). Emotional Intelligence, Innovative Work Behavior, and Cultural Intelligence Reflection on Innovation Performance in the Healthcare Industry. Brain Sciences. https://doi.org/10.3390/brainsci13071071

Brooks, A. (2015, December). Emotion and the Art of Negotiation. Harvard Business Review. https://hbr.org/2015/12/emotion-and-the-art-of-negotiation

Callahan, D. (2021, November 10). Writing Subtext in Dialogue. The Startup. https://medium.com/swlh/writing-subtext-in-dialogue-448b1d3884f2

Cherry, K. (2019). What's Really Happening When You Have a Freudian Slip. Verywell Mind. https://www.verywellmind.com/what-is-a-freudian-slip-2795851

Cherry, K. (2023, December 31). 5 Key Components of Emotional Intelligence. Verywell Mind. https://www.verywellmind.com/components-of-emotional-intelligence-2795438

Clarke, J. (2023, March 1). How Empathy Can Improve Your Relationships. Verywell Mind. https://www.verywellmind.com/cognitive-and-emotional-empathy-4582389

Communication: The Importance of Context - Engaged. (2016, August 17). Engagedhr.com. https://engagedhr.com/2016/08/the-importance-of-context/

Cromarty, C. (2021, June 2). How to adapt communication for cultural differences, and why is it so important? EW Group. https://theewgroup.com/us/blog/adapt-communication-cultural-differences/

Cuncic, A. (2024, February 12). 7 active listening techniques for better communication. Verywell Mind. https://www.verywellmind.com/what-is-active-listening-3024343

Drew (PhD), C. (2023, September 19). Context in Communication: 10 Important Types with Examples. Helpfulprofessor.com. https://helpfulprofessor.com/context-in-communication/

Ervasti, M., Kallio, J., Määttänen, I., Mäntyjärvi, J., & Jokela, M. (2019, May 13). Influence of Personality and Differences in Stress Processing Among Finnish Students on Interest to Use a Mobile Stress Management App: Survey Study. JMIR Mental Health. https://doi.org/10.2196/10039

Exploring the Role of Tone of Voice in Effective Communication. (2023, August 21). Everyday Speech. https://everydayspeech.com/sel-implementation/exploring-the-role-of-tone-of-voice-in-effective-communication/

Facial Expressions - A Complete Guide - iMotions. (2023, September 7). https://imotions.com/blog/learning/research-fundamentals/facial-expressions-a-complete-guide/

Fermin, J. (2023, November 30). What is Continuous Feedback and How Can It Transform Your Team? | AllVoices. Allvoices.co. https://www.allvoices.co/blog/what-is-continuous-feedback

Freudian Slip. (n.d.). Www.structural-Learning.com. https://www.structural-learning.com/post/freudian-slip

Frith, C. (2009, December 12). Role of facial expressions in social interactions. Philosophical Transactions of the Royal Society B: Biological Sciences. https://doi.org/10.1098/rstb.2009.0142

Gallo, A. (2017, December 1). How to Control Your Emotions During a Difficult Conversation. Harvard Business Review. https://hbr.org/2017/12/how-to-control-your-emotions-during-a-difficult-conversation

Gillard, G. (n.d.). "Supertext: Chapter 3." Retrieved November 1, 2024, from **https://garrygillard.net/writing/supertext/ch3.html**

Girardin, L. (2020, May 27). The 7 Barriers to Digital Communication | GovLoop. GovLoop. https://www.govloop.com/community/blog/7-barriers-digital-communication/

Guidelines for Discussing Difficult or High-Stakes Topics | CRLT. (2021). Crlt.umich.edu. https://crlt.umich.edu/publinks/generalguidelines

Harris, Y. (2023, August 16). Communication Styles in the Workplace: Gen Z, Boomer & Beyond. Powell Software. https://powell-software.com/resources/blog/communication-styles/

Herrity, J. (2023). 4 Communication Styles in the Workplace | Indeed.com. Www.indeed.com. https://www.indeed.com/career-advice/career-development/communication-styles

How Emotional Intelligence Impacts Conflict Resolution. (2024, May 27). https://demlegaleagle.com/blog/2024/05/how-emotional-intelligence-impacts-conflict-resolution/

How to Develop and Maintain Positive Client Relationships. (n.d.). Indeed Career Guide. https://www.indeed.com/career-advice/career-development/client-relationships

How to Master Sales Communication: Ultimate Guide. (2017, July 5). Badger Maps. https://www.badgermapping.com/blog/how-to-master-sales-communication/

How to Navigate Nonverbal Communication in Different Cultures. (2024, June 6). Aperian. https://aperian.com/blog/navigating-nonverbal-communication-in-different-cultures/

https://www.facebook.com/TheInnerPeaceGuy. (2023, November 26). Empathy vs Compassion: Understanding the Emotional Battle for a Better Humanity. Steven Webb. https://stevenwebb.com/empathy-vs-compassion-the-emotional-battle/

Inabo, S. (2021, May 5). The 5 communication styles customer service agents need to know. Zendesk. https://www.zendesk.com/blog/the-communication-styles-customer-service-teams-need-to-know/

International, H. (n.d.). How to Avoid Miscommunication in the Workplace. Www.thinkherrmann.com. https://www.thinkherrmann.com/whole-brain-thinking-blog/how-to-avoid-miscommunication-in-the-workplace

Jackson, V. A., & Back, A. L. (2011, June). Teaching Communication Skills Using Role-Play: An Experience-Based Guide for Educators. Journal of Palliative Medicine. https://doi.org/10.1089/jpm.2010.0493

Jordan. (2023, May). Context and Subtext in Dialogue: Creating Layered Speech - NN. Now Novel. https://www.nownovel.com/blog/subtext-context-dialogue/

Kanak, T. (2021, August). www.themodernspartan.org. Www.themodernspartan.org. https://www.themodernspartan.org/book-notes

Kermode, R. (2024, March 20). Vocal Variety: How to Use Tone, Pitch, and Pace for Impact - Robin Kermode. Robin Kermode. https://robinkermode.com/blog/vocal-variety-how-to-use-tone-pitch-and-pace-for-impact/

Kubala, K. (2022, May 30). Emotional intelligence: Components, importance, and examples. Www.medicalnewstoday.com. https://www.medicalnewstoday.com/articles/components-of-emotional-intelligence

Lesley University. (2019). The Psychology of Emotional and Cognitive Empathy | Lesley University. Lesley.edu; Lesley University. https://lesley.edu/article/the-psychology-of-emotional-and-cognitive-empathy

LeVi. (2023, September 26). Mastering Negotiation & Effective Conflict Management Skills for Success. Medium. https://medium.com/@peter.law.analytics/mastering-negotiation-effective-conflict-management-skills-for-success-d2e0a77bbe5b

Lewis, A. (2022, October 26). Good leadership? It all starts with trust. Harvard Business Publishing. https://www.harvardbusiness.org/good-leadership-it-all-starts-with-trust/

Lindley, S. (2023, August 22). How to structure an effective multichannel marketing plan | Smart Insights. Smart Insights. https://www.smartinsights.com/online-brand-strategy/multichannel-strategies/structure-effective-multichannel-marketing-plan/

Lumen Learning. (n.d.). *Barriers to effective listening*. Retrieved November 1, 2024, from https://courses.lumenlearning.com/suny-realworldcomm/chapter/5-2-barriers-to-effective-listening/Adjust and adapt communication styles to be effective in a diverse workplace | TRIEC. (n.d.). https://triec.ca/competency/adjust-and-adapt-communication-styles-to-be-effective-in-a-diverse-workplace/

Lumen Learning. (n.d.). Communication Models | Communication for Professionals. Courses.lumenlearning.com. https://courses.lumenlearning.com/suny-esc-communicationforprofessionals/chapter/communication-process-overview/

Lumen. (2016). Cultural context | communication for professionals. Courses.lumenlearning.com. https://courses.lumenlearning.com/suny-esc-communicationforprofessionals/chapter/cultural-context/

Maaike Boer. (2022, June 15). 7 lessons to improve your non-verbal communication. Www.mycwt.com. https://www.mycwt.com/news/blog/7-lessons-to-improve-your-non-verbal-communication/

Martins, J. (2022, October 27). Listening to understand: How to practice active listening (with examples) • asana. Asana. https://asana.com/resources/active-listening

Mayo Clinic. (2020, September 15). Mindfulness exercises. Mayo Clinic. https://www.mayoclinic.org/healthy-lifestyle/consumer-health/in-depth/mindfulness-exercises/art-20046356

MBO Partners. (2022, October 12). 6 Tips for Building and Maintaining Client Relationships. MBO Partners. https://www.mbopartners.com/blog/how-manage-small-business/6-tips-for-building-and-maintaining-client-relationships/

Mental Health Awareness. (2019, January 15). How Social Media Impedes Empathy. Move This World. https://www.movethisworld.com/mental-health-awareness/2019-1-15-how-social-media-impedes-empathy/

Mind Tools. (2022). Active Listening. Www.mindtools.com. https://www.mindtools.com/az4wxv7/active-listening

Murphy, M. (2017). Quiz: What's Your Communication Style? Leadership IQ. https://www.leadershipiq.com/blogs/leadershipiq/39841409-quiz-whats-your-communication-style

Nickerson, C. (2022, April 24). Freudian Slip: Meaning, Examples, Other Explanations. Www.simplypsychology.org. https://www.simplypsychology.org/freudian-slip.html

Non Verbal Communication - Key Interaction Skills and How to Improve. (n.d.). Www.verbalplanet.com. https://www.verbalplanet.com/blog/non-verbal-communication-skills.asp

Norelli, S. K., Long, A., & Krepps, J. M. (2023, August 28). Relaxation Techniques. PubMed; StatPearls Publishing. https://www.ncbi.nlm.nih.gov/books/NBK513238/

Owen. (2024, April 1). The Role of Self-Awareness in Leadership: How Knowing Yourself Leads to Success. John Mattone Global, Inc. https://johnmattone.com/blog/the-role-of-self-awareness-in-leadership-how-knowing-yourself-leads-to-success/

Passive vs. Active Listening: Uses, Benefits and Tips. (2023, February 3). Indeed Career Guide. https://www.indeed.com/career-advice/career-development/passive-vs-active-listening

Pause Factory, & Pause Factory. (2023, September 27). The Importance of Emotional Intelligence in Everyday Life - Pause Factory. Pause Factory - Emotional Intelligence...Performance Management...Human Resources Drive People... People Drive Performance. https://pausefactory.org/the-importance-of-emotional-intelligence-in-everyday-life

Public. (2024, October 28). Elevating Brand Communication: Expert Insights from Impact Authority. Medium. https://medium.com/@prindustrywatch/elevating-brand-communication-expert-insights-from-impact-authority-dd45ec90406a

Publisher, A. removed at request of original. (2021, October 5). 1.1 The Communication Process. Open.maricopa.edu. https://open.maricopa.edu/com110/chapter/1-2-the-communication-process/

Raypole, C. (2019, February 19). Cognitive Dissonance Examples: 5 Ways It Pops Up In Everyday Life. Healthline. https://www.healthline.com/health/cognitive-dissonance-examples

RCADEMY. (2023, July 19). Effective Communication in Cross-Cultural and Diverse Environments - Rcademy. Rcademy. https://rcademy.com/effective-communication-in-cross-cultural-and-diverse-environments/

Relaxation Techniques for Stress Relief - HelpGuide.org. (2018, October 23). HelpGuide.org. https://www.helpguide.org/mental-health/stress/relaxation-techniques-for-stress-relief

Rollins, J. (2021, January). The forces that could shape counseling's future. Www.counseling.org. https://www.counseling.org/publications/counseling-today-magazine/article-archive/article/legacy/the-forces-that-could-shape-counselings-future

Rosen, M. A. (2019). Teamwork in healthcare: Key Discoveries Enabling safer, high-quality care. American Psychologist; NCBI. https://doi.org/10.1037/amp0000298

Saslow, L. R., McCoy, S., van der Löwe, I., Cosley, B., Vartan, A., Oveis, C., Keltner, D., Moskowitz, J. T., & Epel, E. S. (2013, December 20). Speaking under pressure: Low linguistic complexity is linked to high physiological and emotional stress reactivity. Psychophysiology. https://doi.org/10.1111/psyp.12171

Segal, J., Smith, M., Robinson, L., & Boose, G. (2018, November 3). Body Language and Nonverbal Communication. HelpGuide.org. https://www.helpguide.org/relationships/communication/nonverbal-communication

Segal, J., Smith, M., Robinson, L., & Boose, G. (2018, November 3). Body Language and Nonverbal Communication. HelpGuide.org. https://www.helpguide.org/relationships/communication/nonverbal-communication

Selby. (2023, August 21). Developing Empathy through Teaching Perspective Taking | Everyday Speech. Everyday Speech. https://everydayspeech.com/blog-posts/general/developing-empathy-through-teaching-perspective-taking/

Selby. (2023, August 21). Fun and Interactive Body Language Activities for Educators | Everyday Speech. Everyday Speech. https://everydayspeech.com/blog-posts/general/fun-and-interactive-body-language-activities-for-educators/

Selby. (2023, August 21). Understanding Different Perspectives: A Guide to Perspective Taking. Everyday Speech. https://everydayspeech.com/sel-implementation/understanding-different-perspectives-a-guide-to-perspective-taking/

Shekhar, S. (2022, July 25). How To Build The Right Sales Communication Strategy in 2022. SalesBlink Blog. https://salesblink.io/blog/sales-communication-strategy

Sherman, R. (2024). 9 causes of miscommunication (and how to fix them). Blog.jostle.me. https://blog.jostle.me/blog/miscommunication

Smith, J. (2019). 10.1: Verbal Communication and Conversation. Pressbooks.pub; Pressbooks. https://ecampusontario.pressbooks.pub/communicationatwork/chapter/10-1-verbal-communication-and-conversation/

Staff, H. (2022, August 16). What Are Some Common Barriers to Effective Listening? HRDQ. https://hrdqstore.com/blogs/hrdq-blog/common-barriers-effective-listening?srsltid=AfmBOoqmqKYEHxNtaHGEgLf1wbj4HLWI58A1dL1HxJkByALLDspuGfew

Staff, H. (2022, July 19). Passive Listening: Definition, Examples, and Comparisons. HRDQ. https://hrdqstore.com/blogs/hrdq-blog/passive-listening-examples-comparisons?srsltid=AfmBOopFAjl6S9vHm7QiE5p_QKyr_Y8pVY2USxmTut623TlT-32vIA5G

Stanford, C. (2014, July 5). Adapting Communication Styles to Different Audiences. Fleximize. https://fleximize.com/articles/000592/communication-styles

Sudarshan Somanathan. (2024, September 2). Why is Emotional Intelligence Important in Leadership | ClickUp. ClickUp. https://clickup.com/blog/emotional-intelligence-in-leadership/

Sutton, J. (2016, July 21). Active listening: The art of empathetic conversation. Positive Psychology. https://positivepsychology.com/active-listening/

Teaching English Language Learners Effective Communication Strategies for Interpreting | EnglishClub. (2024). Englishclub.com. https://www.englishclub.com/efl/tefl/tips/communication-strategies-interpreting/

The Importance of Authenticity in Your Professional Life. (2023). Daniellesax.com. https://daniellesax.com/blog/post/the-importance-of-authenticity-in-your-professional-life

The Speaker Lab. (2024, June 19). What Is Assertive Communication? How to Speak Up with Confidence. The Speaker Lab. https://thespeakerlab.com/blog/assertive-communication/

Thompson, J. K. (2017). Cognitive Dissonance Theory - an overview | ScienceDirect Topics. Sciencedirect.com.

https://www.sciencedirect.com/topics/social-sciences/cognitive-dissonance-theory

Tidwell, C. (2016). Non Verbal Communication. Andrews.edu. https://www.andrews.edu/~tidwell/bsad560/NonVerbal.html

tsakelson@ufl.edu. (2023, March 13). Cultural Differences in Verbal and Non-Verbal Communication Presented by Marina Klimenko. Psychology. https://psych.ufl.edu/news/2023/cultural-differences-in-verbal-and-non-verbal-communication-presented-by-marina-klimenko/

University of Minnesota. (2024, June 21). Building High-Performing Teams: 8 Strategies for Successful Team Development. Ccaps.umn.edu. https://ccaps.umn.edu/story/building-high-performing-teams-8-strategies-successful-team-development

van Lotringen, C., Lusi, B., Westerhof, G. J., Ludden, G. D. S., Kip, H., Kelders, S. M., & Noordzij, M. L. (2022, September 8). Compassionate Technology: A Systematic Scoping Review of Compassion as Foundation for Blended and Digital Mental Health Interventions (Preprint). JMIR Mental Health. https://doi.org/10.2196/42403

What are micro-behaviours and how do they impact inclusive cultures? (2020, July 3). EW Group. https://theewgroup.com/blog/micro-behaviours-impact-inclusive-cultures/

Wilmot, J. (2024, August 12). The Difference Between Empathy and Compassion: A Guide for Educators and Service Professionals - Choose Love Movement. Choose Love Movement. https://chooselovemovement.org/the-difference-between-empathy-and-compassion-a-guide-for-educators-and-service-professionals/

Wilson, C. (2022, May 15). How to Foster Positive Communication: 9 Effective Techniques. PositivePsychology.com. https://positivepsychology.com/positive-communication/

Woffindin, L. (2024, September 6). The Role of Emotional Intelligence in Conflict Resolution. CPD Online College. https://cpdonline.co.uk/knowledge-base/mental-health/emotional-intelligence-conflict-resolution/

Wonders, L. L. (2023, November 1). Using Mindfulness in Giving and Receiving Feedback: Cultivating Constructive Communication Habits. Medium. https://lynnwonders.medium.com/using-mindfulness-in-giving-and-receiving-feedback-cultivating-constructive-communication-habits-08f1c5b03366

Zucchet, E. (2023, August 22). Body language in different cultures around the world: A top guide. Berlitz. https://www.berlitz.com/blog/body-language-different-cultures-around-world